America's Experts

America's Experts

Race and the Fictions of Sociology

Cynthia H. Tolentino

University of Minnesota Press
Minneapolis
London

The University of Minnesota Press gratefully acknowledges the work of Roderick A. Ferguson, editorial consultant, on this project.

An earlier version of chapter 1 was published as "The Road out of the Black Belt: Sociology's Fictions and Black Subjectivity in *Native Son*," *Novel: A Forum on Fiction* 33 (Fall 2001); copyright 2001 Novel Corp.; reprinted with permission. Chapter 3 was previously published as "In a Training Center of the Skilled Servants of Mankind: Carlos Bulosan's Professional Filipinos in an Age of Benevolent Supremacy," *American Literature* 20, no. 8 (2008); copyright 2008 Duke University Press; all rights reserved; reprinted with permission of the publisher. An earlier version of chapter 4 was published as "Crossings in Prose: Jade Snow Wong and the Demand for a New Kind of Expert," in *Afroasian Encounters: Culture, History, Politics*, ed. Heike Raphael-Hernandez and Shannon Steen (New York: New York University Press, 2006), 34–49; reprinted with permission from the publisher.

Library of Congress Cataloging-in-Publication Data

Tolentino, Cynthia H.
   America's experts : race and the fictions of sociology / Cynthia H. Tolentino.
      p.   cm.
   Includes bibliographical references and index.
   ISBN 978-0-8166-5110-8 (acid-free paper) — ISBN 978-0-8166-5111-5
(pbk. : acid-free paper)
      1. American literature—Minority authors—History and criticism.
2. Assimilation (Sociology) in literature.   3. Race in literature.
4. Literature and society—United States.   5. National characteristics,
American, in literature.   I. Title.
   PS153.M56T65   2009
   810.9'3552—dc22   2009008385

Published by the University of Minnesota Press
111 Third Avenue South, Suite 290
Minneapolis, MN 55401-2520
http://www.upress.umn.edu

Printed in the United States of America on acid-free paper

The University of Minnesota is an equal-opportunity educator and employer.

16 15 14 13 12 11 10 09   10 9 8 7 6 5 4 3 2 1

Contents

Introduction

Between Subjects and Objects

The popular 1899 travelogue *Our Islands and Their Peoples: As Seen with Camera and Pencil* begins by presenting the newly annexed U.S. territories of Hawaii, Cuba, Guam, the Philippines, and Puerto Rico and their inhabitants as the "subjects of interest and of the most thoughtful inquiry on the part of every patriotic and public spirited American."[1] More than a generic expression of the "benefits" of U.S. territorial expansion following the Spanish-American War, this description sets up a relationship between white Americans, as knowing subjects, and Filipinos, as colonized objects, and specifically connects knowledge production to practices of U.S. imperialism by depicting "thoughtful inquiry" as American civic duty and defining the inhabitants of the colonized islands as objects of study.

The connection between knowledge production and an emergent culture of U.S. imperialism seems especially visible in the case of the Philippines. In his introduction to the U.S. Army–sponsored publication, Major-General Joseph Wheeler calls upon U.S. intellectuals to illuminate the landscapes, resources, and peoples of the Philippines that remain, as a result of Spain's "jealous domination," as unknown to other nations as the "gloomy recesses and strange inhabitants" of British and European colonies in Central Africa.[2] In so doing, Wheeler envisions a professionalization process by which Anglo-Saxons uplift Filipinos from the "low estate of unwilling subjects" to the "high plane of independent citizenship" as both levels move in the progressive direction of U.S. political and territorial expansion and Philippine self-government.[3] This racialized model of tutelary assimilation defines parallel yet hierarchical tracks of development for indigenous groups and other island populations and in doing so lays the groundwork for the transformation of elite subjects into participants and collaborators in the larger project of empire, even as they remain objects within a larger, evolving colonial training process.

What is most remarkable here, however, is that the relationship that Wheeler stages between knowing subjects and colonized objects is neither external nor static in relation to U.S. empire and citizenship but integral to the nation's modern intellectual project and social-political structure. To explain the transformation of colonized objects into U.S.-trained subjects, he outlines an indefinite phase of tutelage in U.S. governmentality carried out by white Americans that would enable Philippine populations to "achieve" a higher form of political consciousness. Proposing the "American spirit" that led the United States into war with Spain as a guide for future U.S. interactions with the inhabitants of the new colonies, Wheeler situates "the tribes and peoples" as common objects of reform in a racial category of non-Anglo-Saxons. By calling attention to the potential of tribes in the Philippines — as colonized objects "even more remarkable than those of any of the races encountered by Livingstone and Stanley" — to bring distinction to the United States in the imperial contest, Wheeler also advances U.S. intellectuals as knowledge producers to the world.[4] But he also isolates "tribes" from "peoples," defining tribes as groups that are analogous to domestic Native American racial formations and separate from other island populations that are, relatedly, perceived as closer to the U.S. project of assimilating alien peoples.[5]

I begin with *Our Islands and Their Peoples* because it foregrounds the pedagogical impulses and racial comparisons that are also important to canonical sociology in the mid-twentieth century. Bienvenido Santos's short story "Scent of Apples" (1955) offers a glimpse of how sociology connects intellectuals of color to discourses of professionalization in the context of U.S. nationalist discourses that defined Filipinos as loyal U.S. allies, in contrast to Japanese Americans, during World War II. Santos's narrator is a Filipino intellectual on a U.S. lecture tour in the Midwest during World War II. Recalling the educational emphasis of *Our Islands and Their Peoples* in the late nineteenth century, the narrator is charged with the task of closing the gap between his white American audiences and the U.S. military campaign in the Pacific in the mid-twentieth century, as the Philippines is occupied by Japan and the

Philippine government is in exile in Washington, D.C. As a "beneficiary" of benevolent assimilation, Santos's Filipino intellectual connects a privileged class of elite Filipinos under U.S. colonialism to the mid-twentieth-century formation of a U.S.-trained technocracy.[6] To portray the collaboration between the U.S. nation-state and the Philippine colonial government in exile through their joint promotion of the professional Filipino, "Scent of Apples" brings into focus the pleasure the narrator takes in his official role as representative of the Philippines to white American audiences and poor Filipino Americans: "It was not hard talking about our own people. I knew them well and I loved them" (22). But when asked to describe the differences between Filipino women and American women, the narrator claims only superficial knowledge of the "differences or similarities in inner qualities such as naturally belonged to the heart and mind" (22). What compels his sudden turn to this objective language? As this young, single Filipino man travels to small U.S. cities, giving lectures to predominantly white American female audiences, he invokes sociology's presumed objectivity to situate his "love" as nonsexual and his knowledge as public, cultivated experience and not as personal, emotional, and political. The narrator's adoption of a sociological lens functions as an act of differentiation that denies intimate knowledge of white American women and that insulates him from the racism directed against Filipinos, who are perceived as oversexed racial primitives.[7] Raising sociology enables him to position himself as native informant rather than anthropological interloper while also unsettling his resemblance to the itinerant Filipino male laborers that sociological studies of race deemed immoral, particularly for their associations with white women, and placed at the core of the Filipino race problem in California during the 1930s.[8]

Using sociology as a mode of authorization, Santos's narrator situates himself as the "good Filipino" rather than the pathologized object of sociology's gaze or as social scientist. There is, however, an ambivalence in his self-positioning that registers his awareness of its tenuousness, particularly in relation to the poor Filipino American, suggesting that there is more to the story. Both Santos's and Wheeler's narratives articulate the need for an analysis that can account for the overlaps between U.S. domestic and colonial racial formations and the comparative race dynamics that they generate. Bringing into focus the processes of objectification in his account creates a conceptual space from which we can apprehend the ways that professionalization narratives structure and legitimate practices of U.S. racial reform and imperialism at home and abroad. Both canonical sociological studies and U.S. colonial policy generated teleological narratives that depicted the professionalization of racialized subjects as necessary phases in the ongoing process of American democracy.

America's Experts: Race and the Fictions of Sociology argues that sociology's production of people of color as the split subjects and objects of race shaped contemporary transnational discourses as accounts of progress and professionalization. If politicians, historians, and missionaries figured the colonial policy of "benevolent assimilation" for the Philippines as a teleological narrative in which colonial rule represents a transitional stage to self-government, then sociologists similarly charted an assimilation process that depicted racism as a temporary moral lag in a larger unbroken narrative of manifest destiny. Just as U.S. imperial narratives of racial uplift figured the white American as the paradigmatic subject of civilizing uplift, so too did canonical sociology establish the white social scientist as the arbiter of racial reform. How, in the process of these narrative developments, did sociology's contradictory production of African Americans, Filipinos, and Asian Americans as both racial problems and the professionalized subjects ideally suited to resolve these problems complicate their processes of professionalization? The writers in my study—Richard Wright, Carlos Bulosan, and Jade Snow Wong— worked within a historical moment in which the racialized body was defined as the antithesis of universality. Whereas white experts—in this case, sociologists—were purportedly unmarked and thus not subject to the dynamics of race, sexuality, gender, and class that would compromise their objectivity, the bodies of intellectuals of color were viewed in opposition to such rationality.[9]

America's Experts offers a genealogy of the modern, professional racialized class of color. I examine why it emerged when it did and what it addressed, with an eye toward explaining its intellectual and institutional impact and legacies. The professionals in my study are intellectuals of color who specifically engaged canonical sociological narratives of race as a means of professionalization and self-authorization in order to envision themselves as cultural producers, writers, and critics. During and after World War II, sociological studies of race aimed to produce a common objectivity about the roots of racial difference, but these studies were also affected by discourses of U.S. postwar nationalism that advanced a global perspective dependent on the mobile technical expertise of an emergent professional class. Rather than pursuing a professional intellectual of color as merely a representative subject or exceptional class, I treat it as a historically situated discourse that renders visible a shift in the concept of U.S. global power. I imagine this book as an attempt to trace and account for formations that reveal the intersection between knowledge production of race, U.S. nationalist discourse, and global ascendancy. Each chapter is organized accordingly around a reading of works by a writer of color that articulate a particularly significant intersection of canonical sociology and the combined narratives of ethnic professionalization and U.S. racial progress.

My book attempts a critical intervention through an examination of the imperial contexts in which sociologists simultaneously constructed racialized groups as objects of study in domestic projects of national progress and also promoted sociology as an authoritative discourse that provides writers of color with institutional contexts and narratives that they could ironically use to alter this relationship. *America's Experts* situates sociology as both an academic discipline and a nationalist discourse that calls into being a nationalist epistemology. I take into account epistemological investigations of objectification to complicate strictly materialist approaches that explain comparisons between communities of color as emerging from racial solidarity based on a shared history of racial exclusion and institutional racism from white academic institutions and intellectual life.[10] One of my central concerns is to show how the articulation of a professional class of color draws its genealogy from a range of locations—neither racial identity nor national affiliation—and provides a way to study the unstable processes and intersections that are often effaced by current accounts of sociology's categories. Departing from intellectual history's common focus on the direct, explicit engagements between intellectuals of color and academic sociologists allows me to analyze the subtle intersections and effects of the collision between racialization, objectification, and professionalization. This study does not replace racist sociology with the "truth" of Filipino American, Asian American, and African American self-representations, but instead questions the presumed transparency of their writings.

To show how writers of color give literary expression to the processes of objectification by which racialized subjects are constituted and become visible, I theorize the space between subject and object as "locations," the overlap between physical sites and processes of knowledge production. Prioritizing locations enables me to analyze the circulation of ideas in conjunction with human movement as an alternative to teleological and territorially based narratives that emerge through dominant notions of arrival and destination. *America's Experts* examines the ways that the sociological production of racialized categories such as "Oriental" and "American" develops in tandem with the concepts and practices produced to manage migration. By focusing on the location of the subject, I take up questions of distance and difference in ways that complicate conventional understandings of racialization and knowledge production as domestic processes. How, I ask, did writers of color conceptualize themselves as subjects and objects in different locations that developed in their writings? By highlighting the movements of writers of color between subject and object, I consider their pursuit of what I call an analytic mode of positionality, a methodology that enabled them to locate themselves in a shifting race framework and in relation to emergent global processes.

Where Pathologization Meets Professionalization

Robert E. Park's 1914 concept of the "racial uniform" is a powerful metaphor of incorporation as well as exclusion. In identifying "Negroes" and "Orientals" as exceptions to a universal process of assimilation, Park argues that both groups wear a racial uniform that classifies them, making them subject to racial prejudice in ways that prevent their completion of the final stage of a race-relations cycle that would, eventually, result in their assimilation into the U.S. mainstream. In Park's narrative, the racial uniform specifically refers to an exclusionary biological racial discourse that constructs African Americans and Asian Americans as racial Others in ways that delimit their social mobility.[11] But it also needs to be theorized as a marker of professionalization that refers to occupational status and racialized notions of vocation and progress. I use the figure of the racial uniform to underscore the way that it enables Park to advance assimilation as a universal process while also inscribing differential effects and consequences as part of its extended structure. Although the word "uniform" is supposed to denote a generic, unmarked quality, it actually carries the opposite function when occupied by the racialized body. Even as the racial uniform places Negroes and Orientals in a common category as aberrations to an American social body, it functions differently for each group in a way that Park defines as cultural: both Negroes and Orientals are pathologized groups in American culture, but only Orientals have cultural advantages that give them access to a secondary form of assimilation. Following his comparative and hierarchical logic, Orientals, even as they were perceived as foreigners of the wrong color, could still draw upon an exotic culture as an alternative source of self-definition and self-determination. Park's racial uniform defines Negroes and Orientals as pathologized groups while also charting separate, interlinked, and unequal destinies that double as narratives of professionalization.

Whereas comparative race studies often begin with 1960s racial discourse, emphasizing the common U.S. histories of racial oppression among Latinos, Asian Americans, Native Americans, and African Americans, my book develops a methodology that focuses on the processes of objectification that define groups as racialized subjects and objects and realign racial categories. Diverging from Gary Okihiro's question of when and where Asian Americans enter history, I have chosen to investigate how the incorporations of Asian Americans took place through processes of objectification.[12] This approach allows us to access the contradictory identifications of racialized subjects, identifications that cannot be explained only through narratives that register their exclusions from the nation-state. This approach also offers another perspective to Vijay Prashad's theorization of academic interest in "AfroAsian traffic" as emerging through ethnic studies programs in black studies or Asian American studies in the late 1960s. Such programs, he claims, built on previous scholarship that aimed to include excluded narratives of marginalized groups into dominant national narratives and also to claim institutional positions for its adherents at state and community levels.[13] As important as the 1960s and 1970s history of institutionalization is, it does not account for the ways that intellectuals of color were interpellated by transnational and comparative race discourses of assimilation and racial reform. We need an analysis that allows us to consider the tenuousness, incompleteness, and contradictory nature of these identifications.

Departing from conventional understandings of immigrant assimilation and benevolent assimilation as belonging to different discursive worlds and epistemologies, *America's Experts* theorizes them jointly as universalizing projects whose most salient features are the tropes of education and racial uplift in larger narratives of professionalization and progress. Immigrant assimilation is conventionally identified with racial formations in the continental United States and benevolent assimilation with U.S. colonized subjects in the Philippines. Benevolent assimilation, as a necessary, transitional stage to self-rule in the Philippines as well as for Filipino Americans, sought to prescribe a single path for the culmination of colonial rule that would result in the internalization of American democratic ideals by inhabitants of the Philippines. As Oscar Campomanes argues, conceptualizing immigrant assimilation as the analogue to the U.S. colonial policy of benevolent assimilation allows us to see Filipino Americanization as emerging through U.S. colonialism and neocolonialism in the Philippines.[14] Both cases of assimilation, he explains, can then be seen as having "critical differends: in their limits, promised rewards, and placements or dis-locations for others who are thus 'adopted' and (un)welcomed into the national fold." Just as communities of color were envisioned as objects of domestic reform within liberal narratives of race, Filipinos, as U.S. colonial subjects, were situated as the racialized objects of benevolent assimilation, which outlined a trajectory of progress that would lead to Philippine self-rule. The policy of benevolent assimilation extended, as Vicente Rafael observes, the "promise of fathering, as it were, a 'civilized people' capable in time of asserting its own character."[15] As a policy that envisioned the transformation of Filipinos from objects of U.S. tutelage into "civilized" colonial subjects, it also scripted the terms for Filipino self-definition.

America's Experts investigates the intersections between immigrant assimilation and benevolent assimilation that develop from and theorize the global flow of people, ideas, and materials. More specifically, I draw out the dynamics of pathologization and professionalization embedded in concepts of immigrant assimilation and benevolent assimilation to reveal the domestic tensions and international aspirations that also shape their articulations. Looking at the interactions between 1890s debates over whether the United States should annex the Philippines, Puerto Rico, Hawaii, Cuba, and Guam and the assimilationist policies used to regulate African Americans and Native Americans as well as Chinese and other immigrant groups in the United States reveals the transnational and comparative race dynamics through which these policies emerge. Yet in relating the "Negro problem" in the continental United States to the problem of the "little brown brothers" of the Philippines, opponents to annexation gave expression to what would become an increasingly important and hotly debated tenet of liberalism: an imagined process of educational reform carried out by a white American citizen-subject.[16] Mrs. Jefferson Davis's interpretation seems characteristic of this position:

> The President probably has cogent reasons for conquering and retaining the Philippines. For my own part, however, I cannot see why we should add several millions of Negroes to our population when we already have eight million of them in the United States. The problem of how best to govern these and promote their welfare we have not yet solved.... The question is, What are we going to do with these additional millions of Negroes? Civilize them?[17]

By voicing a common anxiety over the difficulty of transporting racial policies yet unrealized in the continental United States to the foreign "jungle" of the Philippines, Davis figures the United States as a colonial classroom. Invoking the nation's failure to properly assimilate African Americans as a statement of disconfidence in the nation's ability to assimilate foreign "primitives," her narrative articulates the need to develop a more systematic civilizing process that would reinforce constructions of the United States as a training site. Warning against tendencies to treat benevolent assimilation as an ahistorical expression of inherent U.S. values, Paul Kramer emphasizes the policy's emergence as a response to criticism of U.S. brutality, corruption, and immorality during the 1899 Philippine-American War and takes the specific form of a paternalistic and racist ideology of uplift.[18] But benevolent assimilation is also, I argue, linked to larger discourses of tutelary assimilation and racial reform that are not contained to the Philippine islands or to the 1890s. Although analyses of benevolent assimilation have conventionally limited its implications to a U.S. national exceptionalist discourse and an autonomous colonial state, we need to think about its effects on a dual process of state formation that runs across historical periods and geographical territories.[19] Similarly, immigrant assimilation developed as an attempt to situate early-twentieth-century European immigrant waves in a process of social development that would lead to assimilation in ways that were contrasted to and also interlinked with debates over the black/white color line and Asian labor on the West Coast. Isolating the pedagogical projects and educational processes that structure narratives of immigrant and benevolent assimilation allows me to illuminate the racial administrative structures that they envision and rationalize and thus open up analysis of the state as an active participant in and lever of global flow.

The meeting ground between cold war racial discourse and canonical sociology is, I believe, the articulation of professionalization and pathologization as parallel and interlinked processes that develop dominant narratives of U.S. ascendancy. To counter charges of U.S. domestic racism from Axis powers and decolonizing nations in Asia and Africa, the U.S. nation-state sought to promote the universality of American democracy, assisted by canonical sociology's promotion of assimilation as a universalizing process. The intersecting discourses of the sociological production of race, cold war civil rights, and Asian American citizenship might thus be seen as providing the conditions of emergence for a model minority discourse as an ideology that argues the necessity of internal cultural reform for the ethnic subject to be incorporated into the dominant culture while also displacing the social relations that perpetuate material differences.[20] It is precisely this tension between pathologized unassimilable object and model minority subject that provides a lens through which to examine the positionings of intellectuals of color as symbols and representatives of racial reform and U.S. democracy in U.S. government programs at home and abroad. Reconceptualizing the model minority as a broker, James Kyung-Jin Lee argues, reveals the ways that Asian Americans "structurally enact not models for other, less materially successful groups of color, but instead broker the terms through which racial interaction is undertaken, which identities and activities are made legitimate and which are deemed criminal."[21] As brokers, he explains, a model minority manages, affirms, and profits from the relations between owners of capital and objects "owned" by capital by maintaining the social order.

By situating professional intellectuals of color in the context of global processes, I emphasize the constructedness and intersectionality of their positionings to draw out their positionality. Taking up Kandice Chuh's theorization of "subjectlessness" as a conceptual tool that enables an epistemological critique reveals the constructedness of subjectivity and allows me to focus my analysis on the contradictory positionings of intellectuals of color as both subjects and objects. As Chuh points out, when processes of objectification are taken into account, it becomes possible to question the notion of a "common objectivity" and to attend to the dynamics by which subjects are constituted and become visible.[22] Rather than working toward the achievement of subjectivity or identity, I examine the tensions that structure the intellectual of color's movements between subject and object in order to illuminate the specific knowledge practices and power relations through which they emerge and to suggest the tenuousness of such positionings. Foregrounding positionality encourages analyses that conceptualize subjects as interpellated subjects and as subjects that seek to interpellate others and attend to ideological heterogeneity, avenues that Viet Nguyen points out are foreclosed by a discourse of bad subjects.[23]

Conceptualizing ethnic literatures in terms of positionality also carries, I think, profound implications for comparative race analyses. Beyond revealing that African American, Filipino, and Asian American histories are present or operative at a historical moment or in a particular text, I consider how they are ideologically linked in ways that also give expression to the intellectual foundation and political structure of emergent racial formations and configurations of power. Looking at the linkages between the "Negro problem" and the "Philippine problem," for example, allows me to call attention to the limits of domestically focused interpretive models of race in explaining the connections between racial formations at home and abroad. It also suggests that notions of export and import are inadequate for theorizing domestic and international overlaps, as such approaches tend to suggest that the migrations and effects of ideas are unidirectional, contained, and complete.

America's Experts focuses on the processes of objectification in sociological studies of the Negro problem and Oriental problem in order to reveal the dynamics of comparative racialization that structure their interpretive frameworks and foundational theories of race as the stage from which the intellectuals of color in my study developed theories of racial categories and knowledge production in their writings. Intellectuals of color, as Henry Yu suggests, have been "forced by their subordinate position to understand themselves for much of U.S. history through the eyes of others."[24] To extend and complicate this dynamic, I argue that sociologists of race specifically defined this field of interest through a framework of comparative racialization that positioned African Americans and Asian Americans in both parallel and hierarchical relationships to each other. How, I ask, did African American, Filipino, and Asian American intellectuals of color negotiate these relational models? Studying the writings of people of color can help us understand how people defined through the study of the Oriental problem and the Negro problem interpreted sociological processes of objectification and how they used this knowledge to produce a common critique of canonical sociology. As social changes including urbanization brought different peoples and cultures into proximity to one another, the relationship between modernization and cultural difference shaped sociology's inquiry into the ways in which they were distinct from one another and helped to define what came to be seen as sociology's foundational claim over theories of difference. As communities of color became the locations within which sociologists could study race relations as part of a larger investigation of modernization and cultural difference, theories of culture and progress increasingly came to be shaped by processes of comparative racialization. How is the sociological production of African American culture defined in relation to the counterconstruction of Orientals? In what ways were they interpellated by sociological theories of race as well as canonical sociology's institutional practices and presence? These are some of the questions that my book sets out to answer.

Global Technocrats, Ambivalent Brokers

The writers in my study operated in a historical moment in which sociological narratives of race that underscored progress and development also provided the interface with narratives of professionalism and U.S. global ascendancy. I examine how writers of color engaged the sociology of race in their attempts to make sense of expanding forms of postwar discourses of

professionalism as they provided the critical language and organizing narratives for an emergent global order. My book is especially interested in works
that situate sociology in the context of liberal conceptualizations of racial
uplift and national progress as well as the expansion of U.S. universities during the postwar period. Although Wright's *Native Son*, Bulosan's *America
Is in the Heart*, and Wong's *Fifth Chinese Daughter* are conventionally read
as depicting the terms by which African Americans, Filipinos, and Asian
Americans are excluded, I pursue how the texts also offer an account of ways
in which racialized subjects are included, or hailed, by discourses of race,
sociology, and professionalism. Highlighting the joint productions of communities of color and colonized populations as racial problems and objects
of reform allows us to consider comparative racialization and objectification
within a global context. By foregrounding the efforts of writers of color to
engage sociological narratives of race as a means by which to position themselves in relation to broader narratives and networks, I am also able to consider them as social actors that actively engaged and interpreted discourses
of race, professionalism, and U.S. globalization.[25]

By framing intellectuals of color as objects of study and interpellated
subjects of canonical sociology, I see them as interstitial figures that illuminate intersecting discourses of racial reform and benevolent assimilation
that are generally seen as belonging to different epistemologies. My book
argues that Wright, Bulosan, and Wong pursue what I call an analytic mode
of positionality, a methodology that enabled them to locate themselves in
a comparative race framework and to develop analyses of the intersections
between domestic and international formations in their writings. The first
part addresses liberal narratives of race through which postwar U.S. writers
of color seek to understand how to negotiate their construction as objects in
need of reform and subjects ideally suited to carry out that intervention. My
readings of their texts highlight how their engagements with sociology generated a range of disidentifications that enabled them to position their lives in
relation to broader, systemic frameworks and hierarchies, shaping their literary practices of self-representation. As I argue in chapter 1, refusing assumptions of their transparency requires readings of both sociology and ethnic
literature as the outcomes of intellectual and institutional intersections of
discourses of race, professionalization, and U.S. global ascendancy that are
indexed by the figure of the professional writer of color. By bringing into view
the synchronicity between a U.S. nationalist discourse of professionalization
and sociological discourses of race that advanced assimilation as a universal

process, this critical move attends to the intersection between intellectual and institutional racial projects.

Scholars have frequently explained the changing intellectual and political climate during and after World War II in terms of an emergent technocracy that displaced the leftist intellectuals associated with the progressive prewar era, resulting in a closer relationship between universities and U.S. government and the establishment of intellectual and institutional networks for a U.S.-dominated postwar era.[26] Using a transnational and comparative race approach, *America's Experts* brings into focus the vital link between knowledge production of racial difference and the political and economic disenfranchisement of communities of color. To further investigate the relationship between professional experts and the knowledge production of race, I argue that sociology, as the dominant producer of racial knowledge during and after World War II, serves as a professionalizing discourse for African Americans, Asian Americans, and Filipinos and an interface between U.S. colonialism and neocolonialism.

In chapter 2, I argue that Gunnar Myrdal's renowned study *An American Dilemma* does not analyze black/white race relations, but rather develops the ideological and institutional linkages between the so-called Negro problem and U.S. colonial policy in order to narrate the transition from pre– and post–World War II forms of U.S. imperialism. As my reading suggests, the implications of canonical sociological studies such as *An American Dilemma* were not internal, regional, or national, but rather powerfully linked to global discourses of expansion and professionalism, particularly the growing currency of the white social scientist of race as architect of the United States' future. Connecting the rise of postwar sociology and race knowledge to the dynamics of professionalism and practices of self-representation will allow us to see how narratives of U.S. international ascendancy rescript and expand on a liberal narrative that features U.S.-trained professionals rather than progressive white Americans as the principal agents.

As Robin Kelley observes, "'Internationalizing' United States history is not about telling the story of foreign policy or foreign relations, but about how tenuous boundaries, identities, and alliances really are."[27] By situating the sociologist of race and the professional writer of color in relation to U.S. world ascendancy, *America's Experts* aims to unsettle entrenched understandings of a cold war U.S. technocracy as the logical outcome of New Deal programs that employed intellectuals and cultural workers. Such accounts depict the synchronicity between U.S. universities, government, and cold war foreign policy as the outcome of a linear progression from the New Deal to the cold war, characterized by the absorption and recruitment of intellectuals into cold war government projects. To explain and legitimate the democratic objectives of postwar Americanization programs abroad, for example, the U.S. government drew upon "culture and personality" studies by anthropologists such as Ruth Benedict that emphasized a particular culture's complexity and difference from American culture.[28] Remarking on the pedagogical import of such studies for closing the gap between domestic audiences and U.S. expansionist projects, historian William Chafe observes, "For those perplexed by the distance between America and its foreign allies, comparisons between our way of life and theirs provided a critical connection."[29] Theories of racial and cultural differences took on a new sense of political urgency and intensified scholarly interest during and after World War II, but might also, I argue, be seen as laying the groundwork for the emergence of new types of experts, specifically professionalized U.S.-educated intellectuals of color.

My book takes a different perspective by arguing that professionalization laid the cultural and political foundation for the emergence of a model minority discourse. Conventionally viewed as a product of 1960s identity politics that manifested itself in the creation of black studies and ethnic studies programs at U.S. universities, sociology's production of communities of color as objects of study and professionalized subjects, I contend, laid the cultural and political foundation for the articulation of a model minority discourse in relation to black pathologization and Asian American citizenship. To explain the United States' rising political and economic power after World War II, scholars have long argued that a wartime technocracy displaced leftist intellectuals associated with New Deal programs of the 1930s and that this changing of the guard manifested itself in a closer relationship between universities and U.S. government and paved the way for a new U.S.-dominated era. But such accounts have yet to explain the processes by which U.S. international ascendancy builds on and displaces its racial genealogies. Not only have these accounts conceptualized U.S. international ascendancy and racially based social postwar and civil rights movements as belonging to separate epistemologies, but they have also encouraged views of race's cultural moment in 1960s identity politics. The professional intellectual of color might thus be viewed as a historical formation called into being at a particular moment of U.S. global ascendancy, a shift that is also marked by the increasing institutional importance of canonical sociological discourse on race.

Pursuant to this logic, *America's Experts* argues that the engagements of writers of color with sociological narratives of race need to be analyzed as critical expressions of class negotiation on the global stage rather than as nationalist narratives of ethnic development. Using a transnational framework to bring into focus the fraught relationship between writers of color and sociological processes of objectification allows me to open a conceptual space that registers conflicted voices of U.S. empire while also complicating dominant characterizations of World War II as a progressive and watershed moment for people of color in cultural nationalist and U.S. immigration histories. Many of the works that I focus on, particularly *Native Son* and *America Is in the Heart*, have become canonical in African American, Filipino, and Asian American literary studies.

By calling attention to their strategic engagements of multiple, historicized, and contradictory discourses, my analysis complicates their conventional framings as narratives of ethnic development that emphasize the triumph of ethnic difference and recenters subjectivity. For example, my discussion of Carlos Bulosan's *America Is in the Heart* in chapter 3 explains how the intersections between sociology and literature and between immigrant assimilation and the U.S. colonial policy of benevolent assimilation might be theorized as a way of thinking geopolitics and culture in tandem. Whereas canonical sociology constituted an important entrée for writers such as Wright and Bulosan, who had relatively little formal education (and whose works offer explicit critiques of the exclusionary nature of the U.S. educational system as well as the indifference of middle-class intellectuals to working-class issues), into national conversations on race and social reform, chapter 4 figures U.S. universities as key institutions for the knowledge production of race that is central to the workings of power and government policy and also critical sites for writers of color to negotiate their place in relation to these discursive intersections and a changing global order. Jade Snow Wong's focus on the figure of the artist–entrepreneur provided her with a way to highlight the significance of Chinese women to the geopolitical question of whether Chinese Americans were to be seen as conduits toward U.S. postwar progress and economic expansion or throwbacks to the prewar era of racial exclusion and U.S. provincialism.

As my readings of their works suggest, the various ways that they recognize and reframe sociologically produced racial pathologies constitute the conditions by which they conceptualize professionalized intellectuals of color. In Wong's case, for example, contesting racial pathologies enabled her to question the positioning of Chinese women as complements to the lifting of Chinese exclusion laws or as another step forward in the teleological narrative of Asian American racial uplift as part of an emergent discourse of Asian

American citizenship.[30] These seemingly opposite images of Asians and Asian Americans as both yellow peril and model minority, as Colleen Lye argues, are articulated through the trope of economic efficiency. For Lye, Asians and Asian Americans, as figurations of economic modernity, are defined in relation to conceptions of Orientals and U.S. minority groups as primitive and pre-industrial Others. Wong situates the Chinese woman into this discursive web in a way that casts Asians and Asian Americans as racialized and gendered figurations of economic modernity. For writers such as Wong to depict a professionalized subject that has control over her own cultural production, they have to negotiate their relationships to the "community." It is precisely the negotiation of how sociological discourses posited people of color as the subjects and objects of race that became the context for discourses of identity and community generally associated with the 1960s.

For Wright, Bulosan, and Wong, the professionalization of intellectuals of color is a process of reracialization that takes place in relation to poor and working classes. How, they ask, are the differences between a managerial class and its others explained and represented if not through the articulation and conceptualization of racialized differences? Barbara and John Ehrenreich's concept of a professional managerial class (PMC), defined as "salaried mental workers who do not own the means of their own production," seems relevant here.[31] Claiming that the PMC's task is "to define the work of others: to conceptualize and command," Barbara Ehrenreich argues that this form of labor separates the PMC from both wage-earning working classes and a powerful wealthy elite. To elucidate the way in which sociological studies of race shaped an emergent professional class of color, I complicate Ehrenreich's conceptualization of the PMC as an exceptional class to highlight the ways that writers of color theorize their contradictory positionings as managers and middle-class intellectuals. Whereas the Ehrenreichs emphasize the PMC's capacity and potential for eliminating the obstacles that have historically divided working classes and middle-class intellectuals, Wright, Bulosan, and Wong position themselves as writers within a broader class of workers but also distinguish themselves through the type of labor that they perform as managers.

In his seminal study of Orientalism, Edward Said argues that academic studies of the Oriental worked to generate a specific professional role for the intellectual vis-à-vis the nation-state. Oriental studies, he explained, were not so much scholarly activities as agents of national policy directed toward newly independent postcolonial nations. Armed with a refocused awareness of his importance to the Atlantic commonwealth, Said's Orientalist was a "guide of policymakers, of businessmen, of a fresh generation of scholars," bridging the realms of policy, commerce, and knowledge production.[32] In Said's study, the figure of the Orientalist was part of an intellectual and institutional web of scholars in Europe and the United States through which a system of knowledge about Orientals was created, reinforced, and also formulated as a means through which they would, as peoples viewed as exotic and inferior, be subjugated.

Building on Said's figure of the Orientalist links the fostering of specific types of expertise to America's post–World War II global aspirations, Vijay Prashad imagines the figure of the global comprador as a co-opted servant of global capitalism in the post-1960s ethnic identity politics era. Although Prashad's figure of the intellectual of color is a late-twentieth-century formation, it is relevant to theorizing the relations between global capital and a model minority discourse that the 1940s writers in my study also address. The global comprador, according to Prashad, is a critical figure in corporate America's neocolonial plans.[33] Focusing on the post-1968 university, Prashad theorizes inclusion in the form of "bureaucratic multiculturalism," or more specifically characterized by the convergence of discourses of diversity and upward mobility that are in part disseminated by ethnic studies curriculums. As he argues, students of color on U.S. campuses experience diversity in upward mobility terms and are now recruited to be global compradors by Fortune 500 companies. In locating professional intellectuals of color at the intersection between professionalization and the knowledge production of race, they identify U.S. universities as a privileged site of production for the intellectual.

In contrast to the coercive figurations of Said's Orientalist as the agent of national culture and Prashad's global comprador as the servant of global capitalism, I suggest that the interpellations of people of color were complex, nuanced, and frequently ambivalent. Though the writers in my study often saw literature as a means by which to contest sociology's authority and objectivity, I believe that their engagements with sociology do not register resistance or accommodation, but rather the instability of their self-representations as professional intellectuals. The intellectuals of color in my study responded to sociology's methodologies and comparative framework but also to its authorizing function. To address this aspect, I examine the global and historically significant models of professionalization that the discipline made available to them. Asserting their agency as writers equipped with sociology's interpretive frameworks enabled them to emphasize and give value to their interpretive practices, skills, talents, and expertise. It was entirely

xxiv   Introduction

conceivable, for example, for writers of color to pursue aesthetics, which is part of a discourse of liberal individualism, by positioning the figure of the intellectual and writer as a critique of sociological determination and racist limitations. At the same time, however, they could also reconnect narratives of U.S. ascendancy to U.S. colonialism and neocolonialism across historical periods rather than to domestic narratives of racial liberal progress and the fulfillment of abstract U.S. citizenship. To more fully understand this presumed opposition between sociology and aesthetics, we need to consider its impact in relation to ideas of progress in U.S. ethnic literary studies.

Sociology's Fictions

The sociological approach is generally constructed by literary studies as a "problem" and as the antithesis of literary value and artistic merit. Paying more attention to aesthetics is generally seen as the antidote for overcoming sociology's flat approach to literary texts. Within this discourse, ethnic literature is often positioned within a larger developmental narrative that contains a historical past, an unstable present, and a restorative future. In this narrative, sociology is conventionally viewed as part of ethnic literature's primitive past. David Eng notes, for example, that it has become commonplace for critics to acknowledge the sociological approach as a necessary stage in the development of Asian American literature. As he puts it, many contemporary critics in Asian American studies and ethnic studies "lament the field's historical reliance on the social sciences and its exclusively materially-based analyses of Asian American identity."[34] The sociological emphasis, according to this logic, has foreclosed certain readings, particularly those that attend to aesthetics, form, and the psychological. Even when the importance of the emphasis on social history is acknowledged as a necessary and enabling recovery period, ethnic literatures are still seen as incomplete unless placed on a path of progress from the myopia and shapelessness of the sociological to the fullness and complexity of aesthetic formalism. Robyn Wiegman, in her important essay "Difference and Disciplinarity," persuasively argues that "marrying difference to the aesthetic" does not open the theorization of difference as a "metacritical project that transforms the theoretical and methodological knowledge practices of the university itself," but rather as a "specifying container for culture and its diversity." Yet even her epistemological approach to questions of difference locates the presence of the sociological as external to ethnic literatures and leads her to conclude that it is best left behind in order to move beyond entrenched views of minoritized literature as social documentary.[35]

As Eng and Wiegman suggest, the critical turn to aesthetics in U.S. ethnic literary studies has been an important component in attempts to revise the emphasis of 1970s cultural nationalism on social history and social science that generated essentialist and idealized notions of ethnic identity. Within these discourses, ethnic literature is often constructed as emerging, or having come into its own, through a literary critical emphasis on aesthetics as well as the international recognition of writers such as Toni Morrison and Maxine Hong Kingston. Aesthetics and formal complexity are viewed as solutions to the sociological conception of ethnic literature, the argument being that if only we could elevate ethnic literature to the status of art, the sociological "problem" would be resolved. Such concern over the sociological suggests its significance in organizing conceptions of literary identity. But just as aesthetics has not freed ethnic literature from being read as sociology, literary criticism's focus on aesthetics has not succeeded in complicating cultural nationalist interpretations of literary texts. Why, I ask, has the fascination of intellectuals of color with sociology been overlooked, apologized for, or dismissed by literary critics? The idea that an abstract concept of the literary can move literature forward, however, reinforces a false opposition of the sociological and the literary and obscures the historical and institutional processes—including those of 1960s and 1970s ethnic identity politics—by which notions of literary and aesthetic value are produced and negotiated.

Instead of locating the cultural origins of ethnic literature in 1970s cultural nationalism or in 1980s aesthetics, *America's Experts* theorizes ethnic literature as emerging parallel to and intersecting with sociology's ascension to the status of official U.S. discourse on race during and after World War II. Ethnic literature might thus be viewed as an unnatural category that draws from a heterogeneous genealogy that is organized by its relation to sociological discourses of race. In directing our attention to the intersections between literature and sociology, the chapters that follow attempt an epistemological intervention, putting askew ideologies of transparency and reflection that have helped to constitute renderings of ethnic literature as sociology as well as related assumptions that ethnic literature and sociology have always been discrete formations and are thus discursively separate or, at best, of marginal importance to the other's practice. Situating sociology and ethnic literature as ideologically and historically constituted discourses, I argue, provides a way to question readings of texts by people of color as sociology or as transparently reflecting the "truth" of racialized experience. The chapters that follow situate sociological knowledge production and works by writers of color as part of the same mid-twentieth-century U.S. discursive universe in order to illuminate the ideological links between sociological studies of race and discourses of professionalization, thus advancing a clearer view of how and why these bodies of writing have been—and continue to be—intellectually and institutionally entangled with sociological representations.

1.

Sociological Interests, Racial Reform

Richard Wright's Intellectual of Color

I had no hope whatever of being a professional man. Not only
had I been so conditioned that I did not desire it, but the
fulfillment of such an ambition was beyond my capabilities.
Well-to-do Negroes lived in a world that was almost as alien to
me as the world inhabited by whites. What, then, was there?

—Richard Wright, *Black Boy*

Many a black boy in America has seized upon the rungs of the
Red ladder to climb out of his Black Belt.

—Richard Wright, *White Man Listen!*

In his 1923 appraisal of black literature, "Negro Race Consciousness as
Reflected in Race Literature," Robert E. Park keenly registers the way in which
black literature had become an object of fascination and study.[1] Citing examples of research on contemporary Negro poetry by Professor Kerlin of Virginia
Military University, Negro folk songs by sociologist Howard Odum, comparative studies of Negro spirituals and Scottish ballads by Colonel Thomas Wentworth Higginson, and what he deems a "very good collection" of Negro poetry
in the U.S. Department of Justice investigation reports that followed the 1919
race riots in U.S. cities, including Chicago, Washington, D.C., Knoxville, and

Omaha, Park offers an intriguing description of state-sponsored interest in black literature by U.S. government and military personnel working in intelligence operations and academic contexts.

Describing his interest in African American poetry as that of a "student of human nature," Park positions himself within a group of state-sponsored professional experts reading black literature with "profound appreciation" rather than amateur enthusiasm.[2] Indeed, for the U.S. nation-state no less than Park, these accounts of black literature could advance notions of scientific objectivity while also organizing a hierarchical relationship that defined white sociologists as cultivated experts and authorities in relation to black subjects. In arguing that African American writers were contributing to the model established by writers of "all the disinherited races of Europe," Park frames black literary production, including black radical writings, as stemming from an established "American" process of assimilation that centered on an immigrant's journey to the New World and the gradual sloughing off of ethnic customs and habits. Following this logic, he envisions the African American writer as a sociologically generated figure that is defined in relation to white European immigrants. The state-sponsored studies of African American literary production might thus be seen as constituting an important site by which the Chicago School of sociology positioned itself intellectually and institutionally as an arbiter of African American literary value and an agent of U.S. national progress and racial reform.

On an institutional level, then, such studies opened modes of self-authorization and access to integrated workplaces to African Americans as informants and researchers. Sociology especially was a privileged discourse on race that generated liberal narratives that envisioned racial reform as central to the possibility of imagining national progress and the expansion of U.S. political power in the postwar period. I refer to these nationalized negotiations of racial reform within an understanding or reading of the existing system of capitalism as "liberal narratives of race" for a number of reasons.[3] Not only did liberal narratives—as an apparatus of sociology—define race as the source and figure of conflict, consensus, destiny, and difference, but they also enabled writers of color—as interpellated subjects—to develop strategies of self-authorization that both supported and critiqued the process of economic racial uplift for black subjects. Such economic regeneration was central to the concept of racial reform, in fact. Literature was its material or evidence.

Sociology's production of people of color as both the subjects and objects of race generates models of black professionalization, defined as racialized notions of vocation, which also structure and define the criteria for literary value. Park further argues, for example, that black literature is naturally socio-logical, claiming that it is "more true if possible of the Negro than of any other people, that the Negro poetry is a transcript of Negro life."[4] According to Park, African American writing offers a valuable record, first, of the Negro's self-understanding and, second, of the Negro's development of a new race consciousness or attempt to redefine himself and his relationship to the past. In defining aesthetic expression as the Negro's native tendency, Park proposes, "Expression is perhaps his *métier*, his vocation."[5] In so doing, he figures docu-mentary writing as an inherently African American profession and the Negro as a natural producer of sociological texts. In praising poet Paul Laurence Dun-bar for studying the Negro "objectively, without apology and without preju-dice," Park also claims that Dunbar has moved the tradition of black literature forward. Using sociological criteria to define literary value, he contends that Dunbar's aesthetic of scientific disinterestedness provided him with privileged access to the Negro's understanding of the "Negro problem," which he inter-prets as the struggle to be both a Negro and an American citizen.

Two decades later, Richard Wright would offer a different and critically important gloss on the relationship between canonical sociology, African American writing, and economic mobility. In his famous essay "I Tried to Be a Communist," Wright claims, "I was a Communist because I was a Negro. Indeed, the Communist Party had been the only road out of the Black Belt for me."[6] Numerous commentators have interpreted Wright's statement as repre-sentative of his battle with party orthodoxy and as a reference to the appeal that communism held for black Americans in imagining alternatives to a Jim Crow society.[7] But his remarks are, I believe, less interested in explaining or justifying his Red past than emphasizing the uneven institutional and intel-lectual impact of sociology and communism on the emerging mobility signi-fied by the professional writer of color. My purpose is neither to emphasize Wright's definitive break with communism nor to argue for left continuity in his writings. As Wright suggests, taking up the subject position of "Commu-nist" enabled him to reflect upon, without completely rejecting, the sociologi-cally generated, pathologized figure of the impoverished "Negro." Similarly, the Communist Party, as an institution that viewed literary production as a professionalization process for black subjects, gave him an alternative way of interpreting liberal sociology's nationalist emphasis on economic and cul-tural assimilation and racial tolerance ("Be like us and we like you maybe"), thus creating the conditions for him to figuratively depart from the Black

Belt, the sociologically produced space assigned to blacks under the U.S. system of racial segregation.

I am interested in how Wright's specific focus on the relationship between communism and sociology allows us to see his engagement of the promise of the professionalization of black subjects as a critical discourse at the moment in which U.S. postwar world ascendancy was increasingly being tied to the resolution of the Negro problem. The destiny of blacks came to represent the future of America during the late thirties, propelling the question of black assimilation into mainstream white America into the center of debates over national reform that were also concerned with articulating and legitimating the expanding global power of the United States. Even as Wright depicts communism as generating the conditions that enabled him to reevaluate sociologically produced black subjectivities, he puts particular emphasis on communism's and sociology's joint conceptualization of African Americans as both social problems in need of revolutionary intervention and liberal "uplift" and potential professionalized subjects who could, as native informants and documentary producers, facilitate that intervention. How, I ask, did this contradictory production of black subjects complicate the process of professionalization?

Professionalization, as envisioned by both U.S. communism and Chicago School sociology, democratized knowledge production by giving intellectual and institutional value to marginalized works and experiences, thus broadening definitions of cultural producers. For Wright, the professional becomes both a synecdoche and agent for discourses of uplift that incorporated black subjects into professions from which they were formerly excluded but that also exposed the limits and contradictions of uplift. The professional of color, he suggests, emerges through the tension of being at once the subject and object of processes of racial uplift. Rather than emphasizing the professionalized subject's purity, Wright seems more interested in its "impurity," or ability to understand and articulate its own positioning within processes of objectification. The professional writer of color, as Wright sees it, is not defined in opposition to market forces or by being in control of one's own labor. Rather, he seeks to carve out a figure that registers an awareness of both models and their investments in black subjects rather than to prove the professionalized figures imagined by communism and sociology as counterfeit. Wright's engagement of ideologies of professionalism is not only a testament to its power at this particular historical juncture, but it represents more sharply an attempt to understand its implications for people of color as the subjects and objects of professionalism's expanding forms.

To this day, revisionist literary historians credit "I Tried to Be a Communist" with having inaugurated a new genre of black cultural history in which black Americans struggle to negotiate an artistic and political voice in relation to the white U.S. left.[8] Similarly, the publication of Wright's novel *Native Son* in 1939–40 is frequently cited as marking the definitive withdrawal of black writers from the old left as well as the Nazi-Soviet nonaggression pact and the decade following the Great Depression. Although "I Tried to Be a Communist" is conventionally read as an allegory of Wright's fraught relationship and break with the U.S. Communist Party (CPUSA), it actually offers a detailed account of the narrator's gradual realization of the synchronicity between communism's and sociology's construction of black subjects. Through the essays "How Bigger Was Born" and "Blueprint for Negro Writing," I consider his complex engagement with communism and sociology of race through his figuration of engaged readers and knowledge producers that selectively took up and contested historic and representational conventions in an emergent liberal discourse of race of which they were a part.

The first part of this chapter proposes that Wright's critical essays and novel *Native Son* narrate a less understood historical juncture: the emergence of his figure of the professional writer of color in relation to competing models for the professionalization of black subjects. Situating Wright's figure of the writer of color in the same discursive universe as the professionalized subjects envisioned by communism and sociology helps us to see his interest in engaging an embattled discourse of professionalization in the context of overlapping questions about U.S. national progress and the institutionalization of race experts.[9] At the same time, this interpretive move offers us a more nuanced view of the tense and contradictory relationship that Wright and other African American writers had with sociological modes of representation and the discipline of sociology.

The second part of the chapter examines Wright's struggle to formulate a critique of the modernist notion of universalism, but also to avoid the pitfalls of racial particularity. According to Paul Gilroy, Wright inaugurated a "new kind of black author" and also represented the ideal figure through which to explore what George Kent had famously labeled "blackness and the adventure of western culture." I adapt this interpretation in order to argue that Wright's production of a new type of black writer was linked to his ability to "see" blackness as an object of study and interest in a larger narrative of Western civilization.[10] Whereas Gilroy suggests that this "newness" comes from Wright's open political affiliations and the creative possibilities that they produced, I show how Wright located the black radical writer as emerging from the tension with processes of literary professionalization envisioned by canonical sociology and communism. Pursuant to this logic, I read *Native Son* as suggesting that black writers need not be concerned with portraying black specificity, because this difference, in the form of racialization, already structures Bigger's relationship to the material and economic relations that position him vis-à-vis both black bourgeois culture and the nation-state. By focusing on the way in which the state and dominant culture would perceive a black man in a wealthy white woman's bedroom, Wright emphasizes that racial difference is already scripted. My reading of Wright's text suggests that he engages with the contradictions of particularism and universalism to point out how they were complementary and self-reinforcing discourses. Particularism actually reinforced the need for universalism's emphasis on uniformity, social order, and civil society.

In "I Tried to Be a Communist," the Communist Editor concludes that the African American narrator's poems are "crude, but good for us," accepting them for publication and promoting his work to other left-wing literary publications. Wright evokes the synchronicity between Communist conceptions of black writing as primitive yet socially useful and Park's view of Negro slave songs as "crude and elemental" windows into the Negro's early race consciousness. Like liberal sociologists such as Park, white American and particularly Jewish American writers linked with the CPUSA read black literature as a direct reflection of the Negro's consciousness, but also saw it as fostering Communist interracialism and cooperation between black and white comrades and thereby solving the problems of blacks. Communist Party writers such as Mike Gold interpreted Negro spirituals as protest songs rather than religious texts, arguing that they prefigured Communist deliverance of the Negro from class exploitation.[11] Both sociologists and Communists saw rural African Americans as New World peasants that could, respectively, assimilate to mainstream U.S. culture in a limited way or take their place in the class struggle as the most exploited part of the proletariat. So imagined, their readings of African American writing as folk expression essentialized black culture and made it difficult for African American writers to be viewed as "legitimate" intellectuals and artists and evaluated on the same criteria.

Wright could also be seen as promoting sociological modes of study to develop an alternative to the limitations he identified with communism's literary criteria and vision. For example, in "I Tried to Be a Communist," he ironically describes the pleasure he takes in his work at a South Side Boys'

Club, which includes transcribing the figures of speech used by the adolescent African American boys that he encountered and taking notes on their lives. In relating his decision to write short stories rather than biographical sketches, he certainly remarks on the inadequacy of communism's literary approach, noting that it could never "know these boys, their twisted dreams, their all too clear destinies." Though Wright emphasizes his own ability to gain access to his subjects, he also expresses doubts over his capacity to convey such "tragedy." He thus defines the labor of writing as building upon notes and inventing in a way that reveals aspects unseen and undervalued by communism's literary approach.

But does Wright, in response, directly endorse Chicago School sociology in his efforts to publicly assert a "black reality"? In his introductory essay for St. Clair Drake's and Horace Cayton's 1945 sociological study *Black Metropolis*, for example, Wright seems to defend the authenticity of his published books by pointing to sociological data and encouraging fiction readers to consult sociological studies:

> If, in reading my novel, *Native Son*, you doubted the reality of Bigger Thomas, then examine the delinquency rates cited in this book; if, in reading my autobiography, *Black Boy*, you doubted the picture of family life shown there, then study the figures on family disorganization given here. (xx)[12]

Here, Wright sought to critique sociology's hold on African American writing, yet he also drew on its objective status and institutional presence to legitimate his own creative work. The instability of his relationship with sociology reveals the authority of sociology in representing and authenticating black lives, but also provides the conditions for Wright's analysis of communism's and sociology's visions of black professionalization and production of black subjects.

But even as Wright appropriates sociological modes of analysis to develop his literary technique, he also struggles to distinguish his literary production from communism and sociology. Rather than explaining Wright's rejection of and support for Chicago School sociology as isolated, aberrant episodes or signs of unevenness, I argue that such expressions are symptomatic of the complex melding of literary authority and sociological practices of knowledge production. I read Wright's novel *Native Son* (1939) as an account of the emergence of the radical African American writer as an incipient and fraught professional knowledge producer. As I suggest, this figure is distinguished by sociologically informed knowledge-producing techniques.[13] Before turning back to Wright's texts, let me consider the intellectual and institutional intersections that shape the conditions of emergence for this figure.

The Black Belt

For Wright, Communism represented a necessary stage in the reform of racial inequality and the emergence of black consciousness. His description of the party as the institutional passageway through which he was able to leave the Black Belt, the contiguous and predominantly African American counties in the U.S. South and later the urban ghetto of Chicago's South Side, can be read as a metaphor for the process that enabled him to envision himself in terms other than the prescribed paths of professionalization for black subjects within the racial discourse of the thirties. Wright specifically depicts the Communist Party as the institutional site that enabled him to break with the vision of progress associated with the Black Belt.

But the Black Belt is not a geographical area or political district, but rather an assemblage of racial imaginings that emerged on the global stage in the early part of the twentieth century. Loosely and then over time inextricably linked with black pathology, social reform, and U.S. progress, the Black Belt might be seen as embodying the intellectual and institutional intersection between conceptions of nature and racial destiny. Conflating blackness with nature tropes and imagery advances essentialist conceptions of blacks as exploitable primitives that require surveillance and management. The racial image of the Black Belt, with its historic associations of doomed populations, extreme poverty, overcrowded housing, economic decline, social backwardness, and disorganization, particularly in relation to African Americans, stood as a reminder of the U.S. legacy of slavery and a preindustrial plantation economy. The impulses to engage the Black Belt at home and abroad enabled the United States and the Communist Party to define themselves, respectively, as democratic and revolutionary, and to defend their political vision and global influence.

According to Booker T. Washington, the term was first used to refer to a region in the southern United States that had particularly rich soil and that consequently became the area where slaves drew the largest profits and came to outnumber the white inhabitants.[14] The idea of the Black Belt took on new significance with the rapid growth of northern cities in the late nineteenth century that brought almost 50,000 African Americans from the South to the South Side of Chicago, followed by another 70,000 during what was popularly known as the Great Migration of the next two decades. Emerging out of the encounter between the mass migration of African Americans and institutionalized racial segregation, the Black Belt came to denote the ethnically homogenous and predominantly African American communities on Chicago's South Side. It was during this time that the term entered into mainstream discourse in U.S. culture, signaled by the publication of coming-of-age narratives and academic studies of the Black Belt that attempted to respond to widespread concern over overcrowded cities and urban poverty.[15]

Noting that he is frequently asked to define Black Belt, Washington figures the term as an intellectual construction ("So far as I can learn") in order to emphasize his "objective" perspective as the basis for his explanatory authority and to thus separate it from essentialist constructions of black intellect and knowledge production. Significantly, explanations of the Black Belt also became a way for black intellectuals to assert their acquired expertise and authority over and against dominant figurations of the Negro as naturally expressive. Such expressions of explanatory authority did not constitute a solution, enlightenment, or freedom, but were rather challenged and limited, as I will show through Wright's texts.

With the democratic, antifascist mission in Europe calling attention to the contradictions of racism in America, narratives of U.S. national progress had become increasingly tied to the resolution of the "Negro problem." Significantly, the destiny of blacks came to represent the future of America during the late thirties and the question of black assimilation into mainstream white America moved to the center of debates over national reform, propelled by attempts to explain and legitimate the expanding role of the United States as a global power.[16] Representing the Black Belt proved to be pivotal to such narratives of U.S. progress in the mid-twentieth century. Was the Black Belt to be a relic of plantation agriculture and black slavery or an emblem of liberal reform?

The Black Belt was not only a subject of concern to white liberals and sociologists, but it specifically opened ways for Marxists to challenge traditional liberals and more radical separatist movements, including Garveyism. As many American cultural and intellectual historians have observed, the political left during the thirties was hardly a unified political field, but was undergoing a series of political shifts as the Communist Party attempted to address forms of oppression that were not class based.[17] The Black Belt nation, as a metaphor for black oppression, became the centerpiece of Communist policy in the 1930s and greatly enhanced Communism's allure to black Americans. Before 1928, the Communist Party in the United States had not recognized the particularity of blacks or other racial minorities within the general class struggle. In 1928, the Sixth World Congress of the Comintern passed a resolution that supported the redefinition of the "Negro question" proposed by Claude McKay and other New Negro writers. Their new formulation held that African Americans in the U.S. South constituted a "nation within a nation" and thus possessed the right to self-determination as part of a global anti-imperialist struggle. Following this logic, blacks in the North were viewed as an "oppressed national minority" whose emancipation could be secured through solidarity with white workers in the class struggle. By situating race within a nationalist framework, this Marxist theory of racism was intended to resolve racial divisions within the party and also to challenge Garveyism and other so-called bourgeois separatist movements. The resolution asserted that there was an autonomous tradition of black radicalism, but it also gave support to the notion that black history and culture were hopeful sites of black self-determination rather than symbols of black pathology. The Black Belt nation thesis offered a vision of racial redemption through an emphasis on the distinctiveness of black culture and black oppression. In doing so, it also outlined a trajectory for the authorization of black subjects.

Through representations of the Black Belt, Communists shaped the contours of African American writing and also defined processes of professionalization for black subjects. On an institutional level, the CPUSA leadership solicited narratives about the Black Belt and created publication, public lecturing, and professional opportunities for African American writers. They supported national literary organizations such as the John Reed Clubs that enabled African American writers to develop intellectual and professional networks. At the same time, Communist writers conceptualized the Black Belt as part of a project of black literary reform, encouraging African American literary "reconnections" with life and culture in the Black Belt or southern cotton-producing regions of the United States.[18] Communist Party writers such as Mike Gold saw African American writing that focused on working-class and rural subjects as a logical supplement to proletarian writing, one that could enhance its critique of the Greenwich Village literary movement by fostering Communist interracialism as a condition of possibility for bringing about proletarian revolution and the downfall of capitalist power. Commenting on the Black Belt's capacity to authorize and authenticate African American writers and their work, William Maxwell suggestively notes, "Black intellectuals such as Richard Wright thus had good reason to read the party as both a relative haven of integration and a reracializing institution offering privileged reconnection with the racy vernacular earth of the Black Belt."[19] Through its focus on the Black Belt, the CPUSA opened a professionalization process for black writers that specifically encouraged them to give expression to pathological conceptions of the U.S. South, which was also the territory of liberal reformers and Chicago School sociologists, including Washington and Park.

By 1940, the road out of the Black Belt had become a central focus for white liberals and social scientists in the United States, as well as for African American and Communist writers, including Wright. If Communists figured the Black Belt as a nation that could create the conditions needed to deliver black subjects from nationalist pathologies to the global class struggle, liberal sociology depicted the road out of the Black Belt as a progressive program of racial uplift and moral reform that could help to close the gap between American ideals and social practices.

In my readings of his critical essays and the novel *Native Son,* I examine Wright's pairing of communism's conception of the Black Belt as the racial redemption of black Americans and the liberal emphasis on the road out of the Black Belt. Whereas the demand for sociological and proletarian narratives about the Black Belt transformed the Black Belt into a site of self-authorization for black intellectuals and writers, Wright takes up the road out of the Black Belt as a powerful fiction that allows him to examine the processes that it outlines for the professionalization of black subjects. As an object of interest and study, the Black Belt also brought Wright into contact with black middle-class intellectuals such as Horace Cayton and St. Clair Drake. By analyzing intellectual constructions of the Black Belt, Wright considers the respective roles and developmental teleologies that they imagine for black culture and political consciousness. Depicting the Black Belt as a sociologically produced figure enables Wright to critique communist narratives of racial redemption and liberal narratives of racial reform and to script an alternative process of professionalization for black subjects.

For Wright, taking up the Black Belt as a metaphor for black oppression provided a way to situate communism and sociology in the same discursive universe and to thus call attention to their intellectual and institutional impact on black literature. Their joint interest in and demand for narratives of the Black Belt encouraged him to revalue his past life in the South while also giving significance to his interpretation of the Black Belt of Chicago. Most important, Wright connected the textualizations of black folk materials in communist narratives of racial redemption and sociological narratives of racial reform and called attention to the ways in which they outlined processes for the professionalization of black subjects. He then sought to use the intersection of these narratives—their readings of black literature and production of black professional subjects—as the basis for articulating an indigenous and independent black radicalism.

Recovering Black Pathology

Wright's essay "How 'Bigger' Was Born" depicts the genesis of Bigger Thomas, the protagonist of *Native Son*, and also serves as an account of his writing process, in which he identifies the factors, including moving from the South to Chicago and coming into contact with the labor movement, that led him to see Bigger as a "meaningful and prophetic symbol."[20] I read "How 'Bigger' Was Born" as a text that offers a detailed description of the emergence of an independent black radicalism through the recognition of racial pathology, an evaluation of how black Americans and white Americans are interpellated by antiracist narratives, and a reconfiguration of liberal and communist concepts of interracialism.

To illuminate the specific conditions for the recognition of black pathology that could bring about black radicalism, Wright posits the development of knowledge of racist conventions as forming the basis for the refiguration of standard narratives. Through detailed descriptions of Bigger Numbers 1–5, black male figures he admires and fears and with whom he identifies, Wright painstakingly explains how each represents a different form of racial protest against the restrictions of Jim Crow laws. His sociological construction of black subjectivity depicts individual responses to racism, the social effects of individual actions, and the legal consequences for each Bigger. While the lives of Bigger Numbers 1–4 end in violence, prison, or insanity, it is Bigger Number 5 who presents a more hopeful and effective form of protest. Unlike Bigger Number 1, who uses brute force to bully other blacks, or Bigger Number 2, who can express himself only in terms of his hatred of whites, Bigger Number 5 is able to generate a sense of pride in and solidarity with other blacks. If Bigger Number 3 is a black man who uses force against other black workers for individual gain and Bigger Number 4 represents an ineffectual intellectual who is paralyzed by his belief that "white folks won't let us do nothing," then Bigger Number 5 takes a different direction by using his knowledge to expose the hypocrisy, racism, and social sanctions that enforce segregation laws and exclude blacks from culture and education. Unlike Bigger Number 3, who only uses force, and Bigger Number 4, who resembles the defeated intellectual, Bigger Number 5 uses both force and intellect to challenge racial segregation. When asked by the conductor to move from a streetcar designated for "whites only," he refuses, claiming that he is unable to read the sign that separates the streetcar into white and black sections. As Wright suggests, Bigger Number 5 is exceptional, an exemplary text for the beginnings of the articulation of an indigenous and independent black radicalism, for his skillful appropriation of black pathology; in this case, Bigger takes up the withholding of literacy from blacks and transforms it into a form of protest. Although Wright emphasizes the potential that Bigger Number 5 represents for an antiracist politics that can also generate black collective consciousness and solidarity, he also reminds us that this Bigger probably met the same end—lynching or another violent death—as the others. In doing so, he suggests that individual recognition is not equivalent to institutional and structural change.

What Wright's account of Bigger Numbers 1–4 makes clear are the processes by which blacks have been interpellated by narratives of race that subsequently provide the languages and terms through which they envision their lives. To consider the possibilities for self-determination and racial autonomy, Wright probes the way in which black subjection needed to be reinforced through the restriction of social mobility and opportunity, through segregated housing and public facilities, employment, and ideologies that advanced the racial superiority of whites. In his view, the shared intent of these strategies was to enlist the participation of blacks in their own subjection:

> But, because the blacks were so close to the very civilization which sought to keep them out, because they could not but react in some way to its incentives and prizes, and because the very tissue of their consciousness received its tone and timbre from the strivings of that dominant civilization, oppression spawned among them a myriad variety of reactions, reaching from outright blind rebellion to a sweet, other-worldly submissiveness. (858)

By suggesting that the interpellation of blacks by conceptions of advancement and achievement ("incentives and prizes") is inevitable, Wright also notes that black self-conceptions are forged in relation to dominant "strivings," or narratives of self-making, development, and progress. The multiple ways in which narratives of mobility and egalitarianism address blacks reveal the discursive formation that Frantz Fanon identifies as counterhegemony. For Fanon, the process through which marginalized subjects are invited to identify with dominant discourse is encoded by a set of heterogeneous social practices that enable the articulation of dissent and resistance.[21] So imagined, the hailing process opens the possibility of putting askew totalizing concepts of domination and subjugation and instead illuminating dynamics such as unevenness, incompleteness, and failure. By taking into account the complex ways in which blacks have been interpellated by and also reproduce dominant cultural narratives of race and national progress, Wright reveals the tenuousness of conceptions of race and antiracist narratives.

In contrast to figurations of communist interracialism as a condition for class revolution and the sociological concept of assimilation as the solution to the Negro problem, Wright portrays exchanges between African Americans and white writers as formative to the development of independent modes for conceptualizing and representing the "locked-in life of the Black Belt areas" (862). Commenting on how novels by white writers enabled him to develop strategies for evaluating the "effects of American civilization upon the personalities of people," his exchanges with white writers also provided him with the critical tools and language needed to depict black life in fiction. Remarking that African Americans did not have a background in such "sharp and critical testing of experience, no novels that went with a deep and fearless will down to the dark roots of life," Wright references the presumed documentary nature of African American writing to argue that such conceptions have prevented African Americans from being regarded as legitimate artists and developing their skills and techniques as writers (862–63).

When Wright describes a pamphlet that features Gorky and Lenin in exile in London, looking upon landmarks such as Big Ben and Westminster Abbey, he recounts how Lenin points out each site to Gorky through the language of cultural proximity and comparison: "'Here is *their* Big Ben. There is *their* Westminster Abbey. There is their library'" (863). This scene, and the essay more generally, illustrates a critical theme for Wright: how knowledge emerges through comparisons to one's own context. But what is most compelling about Wright's description is that it calls attention to his own memory of reading the story about Lenin and Gorky ("There is in me a memory of me reading an interesting pamphlet" [863]). As Wright implies, it is his remembered experience of reading that is significant, not only the story. In contrast to sociological and communist renderings of African American writers as conveyors of authentic and unmediated racial experience, Wright depicts his interior life through his remembered encounter with a textual account of knowledge production. In his appraisal, he assigns the same value to vernacular accounts ("Sometimes I'd hear a Negro say . . .") and written materials and thus gives value to informal and unofficial knowledge practices, incorporating them as part of the historical record.

Arguing against the desirability of "pure particularism," Ernesto Laclau writes, "If the particular asserts itself as mere particularity, in a purely differential relation with other particularities, it is sanctioning the status quo in the relation of power between the groups" (99). As he explains, stressing only the differential aspect can generate the notion of separate developments—as seen in the system of apartheid—and promote an approach that leaves intact and unexamined the power relations on which this differential aspect is based. "How 'Bigger' Was Born" registers the constant struggle to avoid the pitfalls of particularity as sketched by Laclau. In the text, reading does not represent achievement or escape, but rather a starting point that leads to the recognition of patterns that, in turn, enable him to develop an understanding of the specificity of a particular situation and conditions while also positioning them within larger contexts and pointing to their implications. What matters for Wright is not a mimetic political identification, but rather familiarity as a form of perspective. The inspiration that Wright finds, for example, in a passage about feudal Russia demonstrates his interest in using the "actions and feelings of men ten thousand miles from home" to better understand the "moods and impulses" of those in Chicago and the U.S. South (863). As he theorizes, focusing on the comparison enables him to feel that he has gained worldly knowledge that allows him to interpret Bigger in relation to broader contexts than his individual experience. Yet he also suggests that criticism alone does not create change. At the moment that massive urbanization is transforming the Black Belt of the South into the Black Ghetto, he points out how it can also reinforce unequal structures of power.

As I have suggested, Wright expresses the need for a specific kind of professional writer, one whose authority emerges through the ability to draw relationships between histories and cultures. But he specifically portrays himself as a knowledge producer in competition with sociologists studying the Negro problem (see "Introduction," xx). Depicting himself as a writer sanctioned by self-knowledge and acquired knowledge, he envisions himself working in parallel with their scientific studies: "So, with this much knowledge of myself and the world gained and known, why should I not try to work out on paper the problem of what will happen to Bigger? Why should I not, like a scientist in a laboratory, use my imagination and invent test-tube situations, place Bigger in them, and following the guidance of my own hopes and fears, what I had learned and remembered, work out in fictional form an emotional statement and resolution of this problem?" (867). By juxtaposing his literary exploration of Bigger in Native Son with scientific studies of the Negro problem, Wright asserts his authority to offer an account of racism and its solution. Closely mirroring sociological challenges to biological and essentialist views of race, his interpretive authority draws from both scholarly knowledge and his "lived experience" as a black man in the United States. What separates *Native Son* most markedly from the sociological studies of race in the thirties is the way in which Wright posits blacks as the central protagonists of American social reform. While liberal narratives of race have traditionally figured black Americans as the subjects and beneficiaries of racial reforms carried out by white Americans, Wright's focus on the different forms of black agency constituted within the restrictions of Jim Crow society represents an important historical intervention in the ascription of social and developmental roles in liberal discourse. Instead of viewing the moral reform of white Americans as the primary weapon in the fight against racial bigotry, Wright turns attention to the development of political consciousness and agency in black Americans.

The relation of Bigger Thomas to other nations and races represents a turning point in the narrative of Wright's political formation. As he explains, "The extension of my sense of the personality of Bigger was the pivot of my life; it altered the *complexion of my existence*" (860). The extension of Bigger as a metaphor for black oppression to other contexts transformed the way that Wright saw himself as a racialized Other. The new perspective generated through his extension of black subjectivity enables him to see himself in terms other than those assigned to blacks by dominant culture, which defines them negatively through the rhetoric of segregation and in opposition to "white" notions of freedom, modernity, and productivity. The transformation that Wright attributes to his negotiation of black specificity with other forms of subjectivity represents a decentering of debates over the assimilation of blacks into white American culture.

Wright tells us that his protagonist emerged from a recognition of similarities between racism in the United States and the rhetoric of fascism in Europe: "I was startled to detect, either from the side of the Fascists or from the side of the oppressed, reactions, moods, phrases, attitudes that reminded me strongly of Bigger, that helped to bring out more clearly the shadowy outlines of the negative that lay in the back of my mind" (864). In a comparison of fascism in Germany to racism in the United States, he points to the Nazi preoccupation with the "construction of a society in which there would exist among all people (*German* people, of course!) *one* solidarity of ideals, *one* continuous circulation of fundamental beliefs, notions, and assumptions" (864). Wright focuses here on the contradictions within a key element of classical liberalism, the notion of a civil society, or an alternative to a hierarchical social order, which both German fascism and American racism hold in common. At another moment, he compares the Nazi reliance upon rituals and symbols to the quest for black leaders in Marcus Garvey's "Back to Africa" movement. Although he rejects Garvey's separatist political agenda, he acknowledges the desire for a place in which blacks could be political leaders and participate in the nation as full citizens that inspired Garvey's vision of remaking a "home" for black Americans in Africa. Wright calls attention to the cultural alienation that has produced a sense of estrangement in Bigger, remarking that "the civilization that had given birth to Bigger contained no spiritual sustenance, had created no culture which could hold and claim his allegiance and faith" (865).

By rewriting the traditional narrative in which America's uniqueness is defined through its opposition to Nazi fascism and Russian totalitarianism, Wright reveals the degree to which articulations of U.S. national power drew strength from the separation of racism from international politics. The parallels that he sees in "the emotional tensions of Bigger in America and Bigger in Nazi Germany and Bigger in old Russia" challenge the dominant narrative of American exceptionalism (865). By appropriating the terms of opposition through which America's cultural and political coherence is achieved, Wright then uses them to question the exceptionalism of American democratic culture through its presumed, absolute difference from Nazi Germany. Wright's belief that Bigger, "an American product, a native son of this land, carried with him the potentialities of either Communism or Fascism" places Bigger within an international context, implying that Bigger's political allegiance has yet to be articulated (866).

Between "Communist" and "Sociologist"

As Wright suggests, reading led him to acts of comparison and revaluation, while humanist enlightenment led him to identify more closely with projects for racial reform and racial redemption. To explain the conditions for the emergence of a black radical writer, Wright turns to the constellation of racial knowledge produced about black subjects. Where, he asks, does the figure of the African American writer intersect with the intellectual practices by which knowledge about African Americans is produced? In the 1937 literary manifesto "Blueprint for Negro Writing," he suggests that the goal for African American writers is to generate a "relationship between the Negro woman hoeing cotton in the South and the men who loll in swivel chairs on Wall Street and take the fruits of her toil."[22] Though Wright appears, at first glance, to be urging writers to focus on U.S. capitalism's exploitation of black workers in the South, I argue that he is more interested in recovering the figures of the black rural proletarian and liberal capitalist as key protagonists in both communism's and sociology's fictions of the Black Belt. These figures were part of larger discourses that worked to interpellate supporters of a Black Belt nation as well as the citizens of a nation that was largely believed to have adopted a course of racial reform. By emphasizing the connection between a romanticized black peasantry and the U.S. captains of industry that were also the liberal philanthropists funding sociological studies of the Negro problem, Wright shows how such framings of blackness enabled sociology to proclaim itself as an agent of racial reform and Americanization over and against communism, which was also asserting itself as an alternative to liberal projects that pursued the moral reform of white Americans as a means of securing the racial uplift of African Americans. As Maxwell observes, many African American activists and writers were drawn to the party precisely because they saw it as a way to counteract a problematic white philanthropy and the negative reactions it stirred up (8). By examining how both sociologists and communists read black literature as sociological in order to figure black Americans as the chosen objects of Communist deliverance and racial reform, Wright suggests that this intersection called into being the need for an independent black radical writer.

In "Blueprint for Negro Writing," Wright offers a detailed account of black literature through an analysis of the overlap between processes of objectification, racialization, and professionalization. The essay is divided into ten sections and begins by analyzing two definitions of the social role of Negro writing, and then goes on to construct nationalism, perspective, and theme as "problems" that are racial and literary, concluding with sections on professional autonomy and an argument for the necessity for writing to take place as collective work. Sociology and communism produced a discourse around African American writing that emphasized authenticity and transparency while also establishing a particular role for writers as transcribers of the Negro's consciousness. In contrast, Wright depicts a black radical writer as a historical formation that emerges from the intersection between the processes for the professionalization of black subjects imagined by communism and sociology. By analyzing the convergence of sociological and communist productions of black subjects, Wright reconstructs the role of the black writer to show how fiction opens a space for the articulation of an independent and indigenous black radicalism.[23] To gain perspective beyond cold facts produced in sociological interpretations, Wright argues that African American writers need to reflect upon the "harsh lot of their race" in relation to representations of the aspirations and struggles of other marginalized groups.[24] On the one hand, Wright suggests that relating black Americans to other political contexts and struggles can lead to a broader understanding of the "interdependence of people in modern society" and that connecting the lives of black urban individuals to the working classes will offer perspective on the majority of the world's population. But he is also, I believe, calling upon writers to reflect upon the ways in which they have been constructed as objects through black pathology.

Wright addresses his conceptions of African American literary heritage by pointing to the impact of readings of black literature as social documentary by sociologists and communist writers. To redefine the figure of the African American writer, he identifies Marxism as offering the unique possibility of restoring the African American writer's "lost heritage" or his role as a "creator of the world in which he lives, and as a creator of himself" (49). By identifying creative agency as the African American writer's heritage, Wright counters sociological conceptions of black literary formation as the recovery of black folklore and southern cultural roots. Instead, he posits a genealogy for black literature in which folklore is an important source of literary inspiration among others: "Eliot, Stein, Joyce, Proust, Hemingway, and Anderson; Gorky, Barbusse, Nexo, and Jack London no less than the folklore of the Negro himself should form the heritage of the Negro writer" (50). Following Wright's formulation, the process of becoming a writer is synonymous with the development of an understanding of how processes of objectification, racialization, and professionalization are mutually constitutive; this understanding then forms the basis for literary strategies of self-authorization.

I see Wright as using the convergence of communism and sociology—particularly their sociological readings of black literature and joint investment in the professionalization of black subjects—as a basis for articulating an independent and indigenous black radicalism. To do so, he has to negotiate the conflation of black literature with documentary and conceptions of the Negro writer as naturally expressive rather than as a self-determined creative subject. Perhaps Wright's analysis of perspective offers the best illustration of the conditions for the emergence of the figure of the black radical writer. As he explains, perspective is a vantage point in "intellectual space where a writer stands to view the struggles, hopes, and sufferings of his people" (50). Perspective cannot be discovered in the Negro's consciousness, he contends, but rather emerges as a combination of a "pre-conscious assumption" and a "difficult achievement." By constructing perspective as a particular problem in black literary culture, he identifies it as a key element in the process of professionalization that also enables him to outline a process for the formation of a black radical writer.

Strange White People

Wright advances a view of race and racism that reproduces and contests the universalizing tendencies of both liberal and Communist orthodoxy while also staking out a position of racial specificity. Instead of positing the recognition of black specificity and self-determination as the ultimate goal of politics, or what Ernest Laclau has termed "pure particularism," Wright points to the development of class consciousness through black disidentification with the processes of professionalization imagined by liberal integration and communist interracialism.[25] As he explains, the recognition of alliances of class and race among blacks and also between blacks and whites will enable the formation of black consciousness and culture or a brand of cultural nationalism that does not require the social isolation of blacks from other political groups and contexts.

Native Son tells the story of Bigger Thomas, a young African American man whose first day as a chauffeur for Mr. and Mrs. Henry Dalton, a wealthy white family with vast real estate holdings in Chicago, culminates in the accidental murder of their twenty-three-year-old daughter, Mary, a University of Chicago student. Organized into three parts, the novel begins with "Fear," an account of Bigger's domestic life and disastrous debut as the Daltons' chauffeur. The second part, "Flight," begins after Bigger accidentally kills Mary and becomes a fugitive, later attempting to extort ransom money and blaming Jan Erlone, Mary's boyfriend and Communist Party member, for the murder. The third part, "Fate," tells the story of Bigger's trial, ending with his execution. I consider how the novel brings into focus Bigger's encounters with members of the Dalton household to show how liberalism envisions a professionalizing process for black subjects as it advances black pathology to regulate the inclusionary process for black subjects.

If Bigger's job with the Daltons places him on the path to self-making and upward mobility, then this process of professionalization is violently derailed by his murder of Mary, his employers' daughter, and to a different extent, his African American girlfriend, Bessie Mears. More than once, the novel showcases Bigger's attempts to interpret the racial logic of liberalism. In one scene, Bigger persuades himself to go to the interview at the Dalton household by taking into account his mother's analysis of the dynamics that defined black Americans as the fetishized objects of elite white Americans:

> And rich white people were not so hard on Negroes; it was the poor whites who hated Negroes. They hated Negroes because they didn't have their share of the money. His mother had always told him that rich white people liked Negroes better than they did poor whites. (36)

By repeating his mother's assessment, Bigger also underscores her focus on white benevolence and its impact on black people. To revise this emphasis, he later connects assertions of white heterogeneity, or the recognition of cultural and ethnic differences among white people, to a liberal discourse of race, which outlines a process in which the recognition of white heterogeneity will lead to black integration and thus facilitate the continuation of racial uplift and U.S. national progress. Bigger's recognition of white heterogeneity, for example, does not change the ways in which his racial construction continues to haunt him and shape his actions. Indeed, the account of the events that lead to Mary's death suggests that the crime is largely motivated by Bigger's confusion and fear over how he will be perceived as a black man. When he helps the intoxicated Mary to her room, he wonders "what a white man would think seeing him here with her like this?" (81). The contradictory impulses that Mary's presence evokes for Bigger articulate the threat that white women carried for the professionalization of black men:

> He watched her with a mingled feeling of helplessness, admiration, and hate. If her father saw him with her now, his job would be over. But she was beautiful, slender, with an air that made him feel that she did not hate him with the hate of other white people. But, for all that, she was white and he hated her. (81)

This passage suggests how a white woman is predominantly figured as an irreducible marker of race and a potential threat to the economic and physical survival of black men. But it also offers more than a description of the degree to which the symbolic presence of white women defined social boundaries for black men. When Bigger distinguishes Mary's regard for black people from the overtly racist views of "other white people," his recognition of white heterogeneity also narrates his attempt to critically evaluate the production of racial knowledge. Even as he recognizes Mary as "different," he concludes that it does not justify another type of reaction from him. What matters, he tells us, is her racial classification as white.

While Wright exposes the falsity of America's egalitarian rhetoric by pointing out the exclusion of black Americans from narratives of national progress, he also explores the terms that constitute nationalist affiliation and subjectivity. In the novel, Bigger persuades his friend Gus to play "White," a game in which they imitate the actions and manners of powerful white men. Taking on the roles of an army general, financial tycoon J. P. Morgan, and the president of the United States, they act out scenes of authority borrowed from movies and other media associated with white men (21–22). Through their performances, Bigger and Gus figure whiteness as heightened masculine authority and economic empowerment through which they are able to participate in public decision-making, direct the allocation of financial resources, and discipline others.

Their performances of whiteness temporarily claim authority and agency in a way that reveals the fabricated nature of American subjectivity. By appropriating the words, gestures, and forms of entitlement that constitute white male authority, Bigger and Gus challenge the naturalized appearance of the white male subject. As Richard Dyer reminds us, power "works in a particularly seductive way with whiteness, because of the way it seems rooted, in common-sense thought, in things other than ethnic difference."[26] What Bigger and Gus expose in their game is the way in which black subjectivity is traditionally defined in a negative relation to white power and agency, thus throwing into question the possibility of black autonomy and agency within such a binary definition of racial difference.

I see Wright as most forcefully questioning framings of blackness in liberal narratives of racial reform in scenes that feature Bigger and Peggy O'Flagherty, the Irish cook and housekeeper. Liberalism, Wright suggests, frames blackness as an obstacle to a process of assimilation that was seen as central to Americanization. The liberal narrative of progress intersects with a process of professionalization at the point where the black subject is called upon to self-identify as the pathological object that will then be reformed and uplifted by white Americans in a national process of racial reform. Scenes between Bigger and Peggy dramatize the logic of racial reform as a counterpoint to communism's view of interracialism as a key component in the class struggle.

By relating Bigger to Peggy, Wright explores the processes of professionalization for black subjects and white immigrants inscribed within a liberal narrative of racial reform. More than once, Peggy compares Bigger to the "last colored man who worked for us" in a way that encourages him to see himself as the object of racial uplift and that allows her to lay claim to the same racial category as her wealthy employers, even though she holds a subordinate position as their servant (56). So imagined, liberal narratives of race position blacks such as Bigger as the privileged objects of white racial reform while also opening new forms of identification to non-elite whites such as Peggy. Peggy attempts to instruct Bigger on the benefits of racial reform by impressing upon him that Mr. Dalton has "done a lot for your people." But Bigger's puzzled response of "My people?" demonstrates that he does not identify with Peggy's view of him as part of a racialized group that is also the object of racial uplift. Peggy's characterization of the Dalton household as "one big family" also leads Bigger to distrust her. Unable to imagine becoming part of this idealized white family, Bigger suspects Peggy as having courted his cooperation to shift some of her work onto him. To reject the concept of ethnic assimilation that Peggy represents, he recovers a history of racialized class antagonism between black and white working classes, articulating a racial critique of reform. For Bigger, it isn't just blackness, but other socially constructed differences that matter in creating disparities of power and economic opportunity. By inferring that the results of differential access are differential opportunities and outcomes, he also suggests that access, as possibility within a range of options, and opportunity, as possibility in a wider and more general sense, are not the same.

Through Peggy, Wright suggests that the notion of shared ethnic oppression generates and helps to legitimate a racialized hierarchy in which the Irish are assigned a managerial role in the professionalization process imagined for black subjects. By identifying the similarities between the histories of black Americans and Irish Americans, David Roediger emphasizes their shared histories of oppression and displacement from a homeland.[27] Yet it is precisely Roediger's superficial assumption of a "common history" as colonial subjects and exploited workers that the novel complicates through the interactions of Bigger and Peggy. These scenes enable Wright to link the histories of African Americans and Irish Americans through the purportedly universal concept of ethnic assimilation. Yet rather than connecting these histories through a logic of commonality that can elide differences, the novel points to the possibility of a cross-racial alliance by portraying the link between African Americans and Irish Americans as relational, or structured by differential access to employment and life chances. Peggy's insistence on an ethnic equivalence with Bigger actually helps to install and legitimate a racialized hierarchy in which Irish Americans are positioned as a managerial class of privileged experts that is key to the process of the professionalization of black subjects and, more generally, to the liberal project of racial reform.

By foregrounding the investment of non-elite whites such as Peggy in a cross-racial alliance, the novel shows how non-elite and elite whites are recruited in different yet critically linked ways by the logic of liberal racial reform. I read Peggy's positioning of Bigger as the privileged object in a larger narrative of racial uplift as a concise description of the interpellations of non-elite whites as agents of racial reform that play critical pedagogical roles by pointing to individual examples of successful racial reform and thus normalizing ethnic assimilation as the standard process for subject formation and Americanization. To further instruct Bigger on the benefits of liberal racial reform, Peggy holds up the example of Green, the former chauffeur who attended night school and obtained a U.S. government job. Though she expresses admiration for Green in a way that invites Bigger to follow in his path, Bigger fixates on the ten years of service to the Daltons that it took for Green to "pull himself up by his bootstraps," thus rejecting the developmental trajectory of self-making and middle-class mobility that he represents. By questioning the liberal myth of self-making in which a black man obtains an education through the patronage of white liberals and uses the opportunity to gain middle-class respectability, Bigger brings into focus the intersection between liberal narratives of racial reform, the professionalization process for the incorporation of African Americans into mainstream society, and the elevation of non-elite whites through the expansion of forms of identification with a white racial category.[28]

Peggy's self-identification as a member of the extended Dalton family and mimicking of their commitment to helping African Americans illustrates the process by which the dominant classes secure their positions through the reproduction of their thought, practices, and social vision. Like her employer's "deep interest" in African Americans, Peggy also professes to "know something about colored people" (58). But she distinguishes her privileged knowledge from the benevolent regard of her employers, noting that her family "felt about England like the colored folks feel about this country" (58). Peggy parallels the British colonization of the Irish to the subjugation of black Americans and in doing so connects African Americans and Irish immigrants as oppressed ethnic groups. I interpret Bigger's encounter with Peggy as staking out points of identification and disidentification between African Americans and white European immigrants, not only to assert the irreducible difference between race and ethnicity, but also to question its logic of commonality. Rather than pursuing an alliance between Peggy and Bigger, the novel represents their relationship in terms of a racialized hierarchy in which white European immigrants are on top.

Sociology Speaking Through

As I suggested in my earlier discussion of African American writing and literary value, sociology positioned itself intellectually and institutionally as an agent of U.S. liberalism. As the official national discourse on race, sociological narratives of race helped to bridge academic knowledge production of race and important cultural and institutional apparatuses of liberalism, including philanthropy and Christianity. In *Native Son*, Bigger's encounters with members of the Dalton household dramatize the ways in which elite and non-elite whites are interpellated by sociologically generated liberal narratives of race in which they are the protagonists and Bigger is the pathologized object and beneficiary of their project of uplift and racial reform. By thematizing the conflicted feelings that arise through Bigger's encounters with the Daltons and Jan Erlone, Mary's boyfriend and Communist Party member, Wright suggests that Bigger begins to develop a form of racial consciousness through his recognition of himself as a pathologized object that will, in turn, enable the emergence of black agency.

The Daltons' "deep interest in colored people" suggests how a program of racial reform was increasingly interpreted as a moral duty for white Americans. From their first meeting, the Daltons view Bigger through the critical lens of sociology, particularly in their debate over whether it would be "wise procedure to inject [Bigger] into his new environment at once" and whether it would be too "abrupt," based on the analysis found in Bigger's relief-organization case record, to "invoke an immediate feeling of confidence" (48; 1940 and later editions). Bigger's inability to understand the Daltons' conversation about him is symbolically figured both as a form of blindness and as a physical obstruction to his development of self-knowledge:

> The long strange words they used made no sense to him; it was another language. He felt from the tone of their words that they were having a difference of opinion about him, but he could not determine what it was about. It made him feel uneasy, tense, as though there were influences and presences about him which he could feel but not see. He felt strangely blind. (48)

Bigger's awareness of the way in which he is inscribed by scientific language calls attention to his estrangement from a position in which he would be able to participate or produce a counterdiscourse on race. When Bigger encounters the language of social science as voiced by the Daltons, he feels its power and reracializing effect on him but is not able to name its source. By directly linking the Daltons' ability to understand and deploy these scientific terms and models to the power and privilege that they possess over Bigger's future, the scene depicts the intertwined relationship of culture and domination. The Daltons' ability to make Bigger see himself as an Other of dominant discourse is symptomatic of the power that white liberals possess through their appropriation and deployment of narratives that revolve around a pathological model of black culture as linked to the notion of national progress. While Mr. and Mrs. Dalton assume roles as Bigger's social guardians, they also take responsibility for the process that is directed at his transformation into a productive citizen.

I read Mary Dalton's desire to "see" and "know" how blacks live as a complement to Mr. and Mrs. Dalton's sociological conception of Bigger as their moral duty as well as to Jan Erlone's view that organizing African Americans is a key to the class revolution. Significantly, Mary uses the language and tropes of social science closely associated with her school—the University of Chicago, the institutional base for the Chicago School sociologists and a key site for knowledge production of race during the early-twentieth century. In foregrounding her desire to learn the "ways of black folks," Mary asserts what she sees as their common, if unequal, humanity in a way that also frames their differences as cultural ones. Her lament to Bigger that blacks and whites "know so little about each other" implies that racism can be resolved if white people become better educated about black culture.[29] This scene locates Mary as part of the University of Chicago social science discourse and underscores how ineffectual her interpretation of race is when seen from Bigger's perspective.

In this sense, Bigger's murder of Mary also represents an attempt to kill off that discourse. Wright literally showcases the university's suppression of intellectuals of color in a scene in which Bigger sees six white men take something from a "brown skinned Negro" and throw him into a cell. Eventually, the man is taken away in a straitjacket, leaving a white man to explain the incident to Bigger: "He went off his nut from studying too much at the university. He was writing a book on how colored people live and he says somebody stole all the facts he'd found. He says he's got to the bottom of why colored folks are treated bad and he's going to tell the President and have things changed, see? He's nuts! He swears that his university professor locked him up" (765). Here, the university is depicted as a knowledge-producing institution that participates in the suppression of sociological accounts generated by African American researchers. The end of the novel gives further emphasis to the linkages between University of Chicago social scientists, the production of racialized sexual pathologies, and the policing of black subjects. By reading the newspaper reportage of his trial, Bigger considers

the testimony of two academics: a "psychiatric attaché of the police department" who deems Bigger more "cagy" than he appears and concludes that he
may be hiding other crimes, and a psychology professor who comments that
white women have an "unusual fascination" with black men and that black
men cannot control themselves around white women (787). Even though
Bigger has already begun to articulate an independent perspective, this scene
implies that he continues to be haunted by black racial pathologies.

When Mary and Jan talk with Bigger and ask him to dine with them in
a South Side restaurant, their actions reinforce their racial privilege. Upon
meeting Bigger, Jan tells him not to use the hierarchical address "sir" and
characterizes their relationship as purportedly horizontal: "I'll call you Bigger
and you'll call me Jan. That's the way it'll be between us" (507). Jan's assertion of their shared humanity does not lead Bigger to feel liberated or equal
but instead results in his feeling even "blacker" than before:

> He was very conscious of his black skin and there was in him a prodding con-
> viction that Jan and men like him had made it so that he would be conscious
> of that black skin. Did not white people despise a black skin? Then why was
> Jan doing this? Why was Mary standing there so eagerly, with shining eyes?
> What could they get out of this? Maybe they did not despise him? But they
> made him feel his black skin by just standing there looking at him, one
> holding his hand and the other smiling. (508)

In relating the unsettling effect that Jan and Mary have on him, Bigger also
indicates that it has provided him with the critical distance that allows him
to analyze his own objectification. Connecting their benevolent treatment to
his sense of racial Otherness leads him to rethink the racial knowledge that
he already possesses ("Did not white people despise a black skin?") and to
conclude that their regard for him is different but still dehumanizing. Though
Bigger does not generate a counternarrative, he connects his recognition of
black pathology to his ability to locate himself at the intersection of intellectual and institutional knowledge of race: "He felt he had no physical existence at all right then; he was something he hated, the badge of shame which
he knew was attached to a black skin. It was a shadowy region, a No Man's
Land, the ground that separated the white world from the black that he stood
upon" (508). Bigger thus frames recognition of black pathology as creating
the possibility for achieving a fuller perspective:

> He felt naked, transparent: he felt that this white man, having helped to put
> him down, having helped to deform him, held him up now to look at him
> and be amused. At that moment he felt toward Mary and Jan a dumb, cold,
> and inarticulate hate. (68)

By suggesting that Jan's assertion of equality actively pursues a racial hierarchy, rather than neutralizing racial difference, these scenes also sketch the emergence of Bigger's independent vantage point and perspective, described here as his sense of "inarticulate hate."

Jan's belief that a revolution cannot take place without the support of black Americans reflects a specific party vision of communist interracialism as an enabling condition for class revolution. According to Jan, black Americans will "give the Party something it needs" (517). Recalling Robert Park's remarks that black Americans are "naturally expressive," the "something" that Jan attributes to African Americans is described by Mary as "emotion" or "spirit" and can be found in black vernacular culture, such as songs and spirituals. Both positions envision a social role for black Americans but fall short of a politics that involves restructuring power relations, opening leadership, and defining a visionary and intellectual role. Amid the backdrop of Jan and Mary singing a Negro spiritual together, Wright offers a close-up of Bigger's "derisive" reaction: "Hell, that ain't the tune."

Jan and Mary's pursuit of interracialism by eating in a restaurant in an African American neighborhood, imitating black speech, and expressing general admiration for black culture makes Bigger increasingly uncomfortable. By illustrating how Bigger's ability to feel like himself depends upon white people acting "white," or in this case, authoritative and dominant in relation to blacks, Wright suggests that black people see themselves as "black" negatively, through the terms of racial domination and segregation. As we will see, the possibilities for the development of black autonomy and self-determination within the limited space of Jim Crow is repeatedly raised through a negotiation of liberal narratives of race and class consciousness.

"Not the Only Object of Hate": On Pathologization and Racial Particularity

In *Native Son*, Bigger's recognition of pathologized images serves as a springboard for his gradual reframing of black pathology. Hearing the legal and dominant cultural interpretation of Bessie's lifeless body helps to articulate for Bigger how racial domination is secured not only through physical means, but through the assertion of particular forms of subjectivity that shape the boundaries of his present and future. Remembering Bessie enables Bigger to recover something he did not experience individually and links his development of racial consciousness to the assertion of his explanatory authority:

He knew that Bessie, too, though dead, though killed by him, would resent her dead body being used in this way. Anger quickened in him: an old feeling that Bessie had often described to him when she had come from long hours of hot toil in the white folks' kitchens, a feeling of being forever commanded by others so much that thinking and feeling for one's self was impossible. (755)

By making a seamless transition from a description of Bessie's life to his own feelings of rage kindled by a racist culture, Bigger constructs their relationship as a racial alliance that authorizes him to speak for her and also displace the misogyny that led to her murder. What this scene implies is that Bigger is able to develop race consciousness and to assume the persona of an analyst through his physical and symbolic domination of women.

In reflecting on his alliance with Jan, Bigger claims to have gained a new type of perspective, one that emerges through the developments of explanatory authority via collective racial identification. To explain his decision to serve as Bigger's advocate, Jan claims that his experiences of imprisonment and the loss of Mary, as a white woman and loved one, have led him to identify with "black men who've been killed" and "black men who had to grieve" and consequently to view the murder case as part of a system of black racial oppression (714). According to Bigger, the knowledge that Jan does not blame him for Mary's death generates familiar feelings of guilt but "in a different sense" (714). He figuratively depicts this change as the feeling that a "white man had flung aside the curtain and walked into the room of his life" (714). Bigger locates his new perspective as emerging from the shift in Jan's interpretative framework for the murder from an isolated crime to an example within a racialized and historicized system.

When Reverend Hammond, the black preacher, urges Bigger to adopt a universalist discourse of "eternal life" as an alternative to the pathologized images of himself in the newspapers, he reacts by throwing away his cross (709). Rather than taking comfort in the reverend's black vernacular speech and the familiarity of the images that he evokes, Bigger rejects the reverend's raceless, universalist vision as a viable analytical framework, resolving "never again to trust anybody or anything. Not even Jan. Or Max. They were all right, maybe; but whatever he thought or did from now on would have to come from him and him alone" (315). Bigger's remark distances himself from the universalist discourse that the reverend represents, but also from the Black Belt nation thesis and Marxist economic discourse associated, respectively, with his lawyer, Max, and Jan. Though he regards Max and Jan as potentially "all right," he also asserts the need to be independently responsible for generating his own course of action. Bigger's independent perspective, his ability to imagine an alternative form of happiness, might thus be seen as emerging through his interpretation of the synchronicity between white liberalism and Christianity, especially the ways that their interpellations of black subjects through discourses of domesticity work to maintain hegemonic discourses. Significantly, his new perspective takes its definition from Bigger's recognition of the ways in which black people are encouraged to participate in hegemonic processes. When his lawyer Max asks him whether he could feel "at home" in church, as a place where nobody hated him, Bigger replies: "I wanted to be happy in this world, not out of it. I didn't want that kind of happiness. The white folks like for us to be religious, then they can do what they want to with us" (778). Bigger's attempt to navigate the investments of liberalism and communism in the development of black subjects suggests that he is both a subject and object in these discourses and might be seen as narrating the beginnings of an independent black radicalism.

Chapter 2 takes up another dimension of the geopolitical discourse of racial liberalism operative in dominant sociological narratives of race by examining the ways black Americans are viewed as included figures who actively shape national and global discourses of race rather than only as excluded subjects. As I suggest, sociological studies such as Gunnar Myrdal's An American Dilemma: The Negro Problem and Modern American Democracy adapted colonial ideologies of civilization and racial reform to articulate black professionalization as part of the intellectual foundation and novel political structure of a U.S.-dominated postwar world order. Such liberal narratives of race figured professionals of color as global symbols of race in ways that displace those professionals' own knowledge production on race while also emphasizing the international significance of their support and participation in asserting U.S. progress and countering negative images of U.S. democracy abroad.

2.

Americanization as Black Professionalization

Gunnar Myrdal's An American Dilemma

In his seminal work *An American Dilemma: The Negro Problem and Modern American Democracy* (1944), Gunnar Myrdal depicts African American culture as a "distorted development, or a pathological condition" of American culture: "The Negro's entire life, and, consequently, also his opinions on the Negro problem, are, in the main, to be considered as secondary reactions to more primary pressures from the side of the dominant white majority."[1] Not surprisingly, Myrdal's patronizing construction of African American culture as dependent on and respondent to white racial pressure has drawn fire from numerous critics over the years. Most critiques of *An American Dilemma*, however, minimize Myrdal's isolation of African American knowledge production on the "Negro problem." Ralph Ellison, for example, offers an intriguing description of Myrdal's study as "an implied criticism of his own Negro social scientists' failure to define the problem clearly," but turns his critical lens to the simultaneous affirmation of black humanity and figuration of the Negro problem as a moral conflict in the minds of whites.[2]

Neglected in the numerous critiques and accounts of *An America Dilemma* is the contradictory way that Myrdal assigns African American knowledge production a secondary status while he also figures the professionalization of black subjects as a critical factor in domestic racial reform and U.S. international ascendancy. In *An American Dilemma* and his contemporaneous 1943 book *Amerika Mitt i vaerlen (America at the Center of the World)*, Myrdal looks to the rapidly industrializing nations of Asia, Africa, and Latin America, emphasizing the benefit to domestic racial reform and U.S. international ascendancy if the United States could send out "black American engineers, doctors, teachers, and agronomists to the developing world."[3] Professionals of color, he contends, are the figures best positioned to counter charges of U.S. racism and facilitate the spread of U.S. democratic culture and capitalism to the developing nations that are predominantly populated by the "colored people of the earth."[4] The Negro problem, according to Myrdal, need not be viewed as a manifestation of American deficiencies or as a liability for Americans, but instead has the potential—through black professionalization—to develop new modes for the consolidation and extension of U.S. political authority in domestic and global contexts.

In this chapter, I argue that *An American Dilemma* outlines a model of black professionalization toward the production of a postwar technocracy that would become a standard feature in dominant accounts of the transition from New Deal progressivism to postwar U.S. hegemony. Conventional U.S. histories depict the rise of a technocracy in terms of a transition from the New Deal administration's incorporation of intellectuals to a closer relationship between government and universities during World War II.[5] However, my reading of Myrdal's narrative suggests that he specifically saw this technocracy as a U.S.-trained professional class of color that could be exported as U.S. representatives and agents to developing nations. To counter the negative image of America that the United States' record of racism has generated abroad, particularly in "colored nations," Myrdal also underscores the need to enlist the support and participation of African Americans and to contain their activities or expressions that threatened the U.S. democratic image. Even as he deems the "colored people's confidence" in the war unnecessary, he argues that the absence of their "full cooperation," alongside their "obstructive activities," constituted a liability for the United States.[6]

Recent scholarship by Mary Dudziak, Brenda Gayle Plummer, Penny Von Eschen, and Christina Klein has amply demonstrated the ways that the U.S. State Department saw the participation of African American and Asian American intellectuals and entertainers in official tours to newly decolonized Asian and African nations as critical factors in the joint effort to advance a liberal process of domestic racial reform and counter negative publicity about U.S. racist practices abroad. This body of work has also been significant in bringing into view the intellectuals and artists who participated in these tours as social actors rather than objects in hegemonic discourses. Situating *An American Dilemma* in relation to cold war racial discourses has also enabled critics to point out the global and cold war pressures that animate Myrdal's model for domestic U.S. race reform. Through their focus on the official tours, these studies have illuminated the ways that the U.S. state actively restricted the mobility and expressions of African American intellectuals, including W. E. B. Du Bois and Paul Robeson, but also, as Jodi Melamed points out, encouraged "black people to prioritize an identification with America above all identifications, racial antiracist, internationalist, or diasporic."[7] Understanding how these intellectuals, entertainers, and public figures of color interpreted, negotiated, and contested their positionings in relation to the U.S. government's cold war agenda has illuminated an important archive of critique and developing understandings of a model minority discourse as emerging through a discourse of U.S. nationalism.

Yet the incorporations of black professionals cannot be theorized on an individual level only or in relation to the nation-state, but need to be analyzed as part of a broader discourse of black professionalization as it intersects with colonial discourses of racial uplift and civilization. Black professionalization, as Myrdal suggests, is not an effect or external feature of the emergent U.S.-dominated global order, but rather part of its intellectual foundation and political structure. This chapter reads *An American Dilemma* as pursuing a vision of U.S. ascension that exploits black professionals as global symbols of race while also displacing African American knowledge production on the Negro problem intellectually and institutionally. I begin by discussing Myrdal's emphasis on cultural education as a central component in domestic race reform and U.S. postwar hegemony. To situate his conceptualization of Americanization education within a civilizationist discourse of race, I discuss how it draws upon and extends a model of tutelary assimilation employed in the U.S. colonial policy of benevolent assimilation in the Philippines. By connecting Myrdal's 1940s model for black professionalization to the form of Americanization education outlined in a late-nineteenth-century discourse of benevolent assimilation, this chapter complicates domestically based understandings of *An American Dilemma* as a white/black U.S. race-relations study and also shifts the traditional frame of reference for benevolent assimilation from the 1890s and as grounded in the territory of the Philippines to an extraterritorial discourse that links pre- and post–World War II forms of U.S. imperialism.

The concluding sections of the chapter situate Myrdal's advocacy of social engineering as a scientific process that would improve the status of African Americans. Progressives including Myrdal defined social engineering as a broad range of activities in education, social welfare, economics, social planning, and eugenics (Jackson, 374, n. 13) and as the "supreme task of social science."[8] I examine his conceptualization of education as an integral component of social engineering that would facilitate the process of assimilation and assist blacks in losing the "distinctive cultural traits" that were preventing them from taking up dominant American cultural practices as embodied by the American Creed, an abstract set of precepts or a spirit with which Americans and non-Americans are invited to identify. Unlike biological notions of American identity, the American Creed represents a form of nationalist affiliation that turns upon a "common sharing in both the consciousness of sins and the devotion to high ideals" (22).

I read *An American Dilemma* as the text that advances black professionalization as the solution to the Negro problem and condition for U.S. global ascension. Broadly viewed as the authoritative study of U.S. race relations in the mid-twentieth century, the study spans more than one thousand pages, beginning with an account of the English and European origins of American culture before shifting to a separate account of African American social practices and culminating in recommendations for a national policy on race. The first volume connects American origins to the Negro problem through an examination of theories of race and racism, black population growth and migration to the North, the economic and labor systems of slavery and southern agriculture, the black professional classes, and the impact of World War II on African Americans. In advocating for the assimilation of blacks to American cultural values, the second volume of the study develops a discourse of pathology by emphasizing the cultural distinctiveness of African Americans.

If the numerous critical accounts of *An American Dilemma* agree on one thing, it is that the study represents a watershed in official U.S. liberal discourse on race. To begin, the Carnegie Corporation's decision to commission a "comprehensive study of the Negro problem" and to hire Myrdal, a Swedish economist and sociologist, to head the project is frequently portrayed as a high point in the intellectual assault on racism. Perceived by the Carnegie Corporation board as a neutral outsider to U.S. racial politics, Myrdal was charged with registering the negative consequences of U.S. racist practices for African American communities and issuing an official repudiation of racism by emphasizing its implications for national progress and the U.S. democratic image abroad. In his foreword to *An American Dilemma*, corporation president Frederick P. Keppel summed up the wartime cultural climate as a time "when the eyes of men of all races the world over are turned upon us to see how the people of the most powerful of the United Nations are dealing at home with a major problem of race relations" (lviii). The international audience that Keppel dramatically portrays also testifies to the way in which U.S. global power had been called into question by the increasing visibility of its racist practices at home. Amid Axis and Soviet propaganda intended to highlight U.S. domestic racial problems and undermine its claims of democratic and cultural superiority, racial reform or the resolution of the Negro problem became critical to the United States' image and its international aspirations. Toward this goal, Keppel endorsed Myrdal's view that the United States needed to undertake the scientific approach of social engineering to better the social position of blacks, citing the increasing sense of militancy among blacks as evidence that the state of race relations would have a profound impact on U.S. postwar diplomacy.[9]

An American Dilemma is seen by many scholars as signaling a "new liberal orthodoxy on race" through its official repudiation of biological theories of race and advancement of a progressive, culturally based concept of ethnicity during World War II. "Myrdal's opus," sociologist Stephen Steinberg states, "served as an epitaph to the old racial order and as an intellectual baptism for a new racial status quo—the one that evolved during the first post-war decade and that would persist until it came under challenge from a grassroots protest movement."[10] Widely regarded as the authoritative mid-twentieth-century study of race relations, An American Dilemma is widely seen by critics, including Steinberg, as having been extinguished by its failure to predict the racially based social movements of the 1960s. From a slightly different angle, Myrdal's study is also seen as having institutionalized a framework for the study of race and racism. Historian Matthew Jacobsen argues, for example, that the appearance of An American Dilemma in 1944 marked the "beginning of the end" of alternatives to the black/white race model, particularly pluralist conceptions of America as a diverse nation that receded from public view as well as discourses of race, power, and social policy.[11] In his important study of whiteness as a racial category, Jacobsen claims that Myrdal's study reinforced a black/white model of race relations by establishing a "simpler" racial framework in which whiteness represented the American norm and "the Negro" represented the singular racial problem to be solved.

An American Dilemma is also frequently invoked for its impact on the Brown v. Board of Education decision, the famous 1954 school desegregation case. Supreme Court Chief Justice Earl Warren drew from Myrdal's study to support the view that segregated schools were inherently unequal.[12] From this perspective, the study is credited with undermining the intellectual underpinnings of racial segregation and opening the way for legal changes that would enable African Americans to "achieve" protection under U.S. laws.[13] Yet the study's treatment of education goes beyond its impact on legal cases on racial segregation. Education is central to Myrdal's understanding of the American Creed as a concept embedded in a discourse of Americanization education, the broad effort to strengthen the U.S. national value system at both the institutional and individual levels.[14] Myrdal specifically imagines Americanization education as taking the form of a broad program of cultural uplift carried out by white Americans through institutions such as church, schools, and literacy projects as well as through what he calls passive mass education or media such as radio, newspapers and popular magazines, and movies. So imagined, this program would transform African Americans into rational subjects and prepare them for the responsibilities of U.S. citizenship as part of a broader, evolving program of American civilization.

In Myrdal's narrative, the American Creed revolves around a process of cultural education that takes the form of tutelage in national values embodied by the creed. Imagined as a form of Americanization, this educational process is also the mode by which black professionalization takes place, as a component of the universal process of assimilation in Myrdal's study. In the first chapter of *An American Dilemma*, "American Ideals and the American Conscience," Myrdal depicts the American Creed as a "spirit" that can unite disparate groups and interests under a common set of ideals.[15] To close the gap between egalitarian ideals and practices, Myrdal explains, white Americans need to strengthen and expand their understanding of the creed's political scope by including African Americans. The American Creed, according to Myrdal, is accessible to "Americans of all national origins, classes, regions, creeds, and colors" and is widely recognized as the "highest law of the land" and a set of principles that ought to rule, even though its egalitarian principles have not been fully realized in social practices (3–4). Although the American Creed privileges a particular definition of national origins and development, it also generates limited forms of identification and separate development trajectories for nonwhites and "other Americans" as groups that cannot identify with the history of the creed through descent or cultural heritage, thus including rather than excluding them in the creed's political culture. By portraying U.S. national culture as the logical outcome of a civilizing English presence, Myrdal constructs order, rationality, and egalitarianism as English traits that were first "cultivated by English law" and, over time, nurtured in the United States (12). Through the metaphor of English law lending order to the American wilderness, Myrdal defines democracy and egalitarianism as the natural preserve of Anglo-American culture. By defining the Negro problem as a "moral lag" on the part of white Americans, Myrdal argues that white Americans need to include African Americans in this culture of the American Creed to ignite the process of racial reform that would restore the U.S. nation to its path of progress toward international leadership.

Located at the center of the creed, Americanization education produces a shared political culture in a way that exemplifies the "national experience of uniting racial and cultural diversities and a national theory, if no consistent practice, of freedom and equality for all."[16] To emphasize the international significance of black professionalization, Myrdal theorizes African Americans as the objects of racial reform carried out by white Americans as well as the subjects of U.S. imperialism, implying that they could be "made more American" through cultural education and prepared for global export as a skilled labor force and, as part of this process, be transformed into the iconic figures of American democratic progress.

Where Civilization Meets Professionalization

In 1935, Newton D. Baker, a Carnegie Corporation trustee, urged the board to commission a comprehensive study of the Negro problem that would lay the groundwork for an extended civilizing mission carried out by white Americans. For Baker, African slavery was a civilizing process that effectively transformed "wild savages" into "useful laborers." Slavery, he implied, was a standard form of incorporation in a civilization project rooted in the benevolent interest of white Americans. Pursuant to this logic, he advocated the reintroduction of African Americans into a process of rationalization that combined cultural uplift with their transformation into an exploitable laboring class.[17] By figuring slavery as an "unparalleled achievement" in U.S. history, Baker claimed that its transformative process of uplift could be logically extended to a mid-twentieth-century process of race reform. Through his administrative work with Cleveland relief organizations, Baker develops an understanding of cultural reform as a process intended to eradicate cultural habits brought by black migrants from the South that were, as he put it, "better adapted to cabin life in the palmetto swamps than they were to the sanitary and hygienic needs of congested life in an industrial city." Baker thus frames the Negro problem in northern cities in terms of a white/black racial framework, but also situates it within a racialized, imperial discourse of civilization.

I see Myrdal's emphasis on education and professionalization in *An American Dilemma* as emerging from the ideological linkages and institutional webs through which Baker's civilizationist formulation of the Negro problem develops. The Carnegie Corporation relies heavily upon Baker's conceptualization of the Negro problem in formulating the study's framework and goals. In explaining the Carnegie board's decision to support Baker's proposal, Keppel, as corporation president, pointed to Baker's domestic and international record in managing racial issues as city solicitor and mayor of Cleveland and secretary of war under President Woodrow Wilson, emphasizing his management experience with growing African American communities in northern urban areas as well as with related groups, or the "special problems which the presence of the Negro element in our population inevitably creates in time of national crisis" (vi).

By invoking U.S. colonial discourse, my goal is not to locate it as the origin for the formulation of the Negro problem in *An American Dilemma*. Rather, I want to show how Myrdal's conceptualization of Americanization as an education-based process of black professionalization engages and extends the pedagogical impulses and structure of tutelary assimilation developed in the U.S. colonial policy of benevolent assimilation in the Philippines. Baker's emphasis on cultural uplift for black migrants from the South resonates with his characterization of U.S. colonial policy in the Philippines as a "progressive process of tutelage, assimilation, and building of capacity."[18] Bringing the connection between U.S. colonial tutelage and Myrdal's model for black professionalization into focus reveals its articulation of a managerial hierarchy that involves funding from northern philanthropists, local supervision by white southerners, and general management by the federal government. Myrdal's 1944 view of assimilation as an inevitable yet gradual solution to the Negro problem clearly resonates with the gradualist process imagined for Philippine independence. As secretary of war, Baker handled the request by Philippine president Manuel Quezon to grant the Philippines an "early independence" based on Filipino loyalty and military support to the United States during World War I and demonstrated capacities for self-government as the condition of national sovereignty stipulated in the Jones Act. During a meeting with Baker in 1919, Quezon drew attention to the contradiction between U.S. colonialism in Asia and calls for self-determination in Germany and the Ottoman Empire, arguing that U.S. recognition of Philippine independence presented an ideal way of displaying U.S. moral superiority and urging Baker to show the world that the United States is a "liberating rather than a conquering nation."[19] Ultimately, Baker refused Quezon's request for Philippine independence. Urging Quezon to tell Filipinos to exercise "patience," he claimed that the time for the Philippines to sever the remaining political tie to the United States had almost but not quite yet arrived. Myrdal extends Baker's emphasis on a gradualist process for the assimilation of alien groups, noting that Americans "see obstacles; they emphasize the religious and racial differences, they believe it will take a long time. But they assume that it is going to happen, and do not have, on the whole, strong objections to it— provided it is located in a distant future" (53).

For Myrdal, absorbing groups generally thought to be unassimilable is the best strategy for ensuring America's "international prestige, power, and future security" and validating the project of American civilization (1016).[20] As a project that peddles civilization as black professionalization, *An American Dilemma* develops discourses of Americanization education and social engineering that are also intended as antidotes for black militancy. Rather than treating Myrdal's education-based theory of Americanization as just another of the many subjects that the study takes up, I propose that it functions as the central organizing principle for his vision of the postwar U.S. nation. More precisely, Myrdal defines the cultural values embedded in the American Creed as having a natural cultural link with U.S. cultural origins in English law and the European Enlightenment for white Anglo-European Americans in a way that also designates a secondary form of cultural identification for nonwhite Americans. The creed might thus be seen as installing dynamics of inclusion and inferiorization that carry implications beyond Myrdal's study and time.

Inferiorization as Inclusionary Practice

Composed of research memoranda from several African American intellectuals who were part of the Chicago School of sociology, *An American Dilemma* is a compelling example of a study that depended heavily on the access and intellectual labor of black scholars. The study and its foundational theories of race are built on the work of at least thirty African American scholars, including Horace Cayton, St. Clair Drake, Ralph Bunche, E. Franklin Frazier, and Charles Johnson. At the same time, the study discredited African American race knowledge by portraying African Americans as weak, opportunistic, and unstable in their convictions and commitment to strategy rather than as original thinkers and self-reliant subjects (782). Additionally, Myrdal argues that black intellectuals do not possess the necessary distinction from the black masses, in contrast to the clear separation of white intellectuals from white working classes. By generating a discourse of black pathology, the study established the authority of white social scientists as racialized bodies that were viewed as unmarked and possessing a natural objectivity that was a necessary component of scientific analysis and disenfranchised African Americans as knowledge producers both intellectually and institutionally.

In portraying Negro thought as a "fluid and amorphous mass of all sorts of embryos of thoughts," Myrdal constructs it as the antithesis of "American" rationality. As he contends, "Negro popular theories, or lack of theories, about the larger society" portray blacks as "emotional" and "unstable," a perception reinforced by, among other things, their cultural production.[21] Rejecting the widely held belief by white Americans that "emotionalism" and "irrationality" are biologically rooted in blacks, he argues instead that such characteristics are the outcome of the exclusion of blacks from identification with the American Creed (785). Describing African American knowledge production as "derivative, or secondary, thinking," he also pegs it as the outcome of "caste exclusion" and thus as a response to whites: "Negro thinking is almost completely determined by white opinions—negatively and positively.... Negro thinking develops upon the presuppositions of white thinking. In its purest protest form it is a blunt denial and refutation of white opinions.... Negro thinking seldom moves outside the orbit fixed by the whites' conceptions about the Negroes and about caste" (784). Myrdal thus figures the development of black identification with the national ethos of the American Creed as critical to the transformation of blacks into rational subjects and global citizens (783).

Myrdal saw black professionalization and middle-class formation as key components in the expansion of the American Creed at home and abroad as well as in the spread of U.S. capitalism. Bolstering Negro business professions, he argued, would assist the resolution of the Negro problem through the "development of a Negro middle class of landowners, businessmen, and professionals" (800). Incorporating African Americans into an American business culture, he implies, would "stimulate the Negro's initiative, give him valuable training and experience, increase his self-confidence, increase his wealth, create a relatively secure middle and upper-middle class, give employment to Negroes in the lower classes, and provide a reservoir of resources which can be used in competition with the whites" (801).[22] If blacks would adopt "white" ideals about capital and production, according to Myrdal, it would be possible to include them in U.S. economic progress and thus speed the process of assimilation.

Black professionalization, according to Myrdal, was a socially engineered solution to the Negro problem and hence constituted a break with fatalistic theories held by Robert Park and other sociologists. But he also retained

Park's figuration of African Americans as biologically incapable of objectivity and hence as the antithesis of scientific rationality. In his theory of racial temperament, Park describes the Negro as characterized by a "natural attachment to known familiar objects, places, and persons" and also "preadapted to conservatism and to local and personal loyalties," in contrast to groups such as white Americans and Japanese Americans that possess the universal human tendency for racial antipathy toward those who appear racially different than one's own. Given the Negro's tendency toward local and personal loyalty, Park suggests, the system of slavery provided the Negro with the proper "vocation" to suit his racial temperament.[23]

Of Myrdal's critics, Black Marxists were among the only ones to call attention to his conceptualization of education and social engineering, which they deemed ineffective solutions to racism. In *The Negro People in America: A Critique of Gunnar Myrdal's An American Dilemma*, a book-length critique of Myrdal's study, Herbert Aptheker denounced Myrdal's focus on morality and deemed his proposal of "elite-directed social engineering" as an inadequate antiracism strategy.[24] Doxey Wilkerson, a former contributor to *An American Dilemma* whose essay on black education was removed for "Marxist bias," criticized Myrdal's vision of a "long, gradual, and never ending process of 'education' as a solution to racism, rather than examining the economic causes of racism."[25] Black Marxist intellectuals such as Herbert Aptheker, Doxey Wilkerson, and Oliver Cox deserve credit for picking up on Myrdal's specific emphasis on education as a critical part of his vision of elite-directed social engineering. In doing so, they opened the possibility of reading Myrdal's study for its inclusive gestures—how, they asked, did Myrdal theorize blacks as included subjects in, to borrow from Wilkerson, the "never ending process of education" that he saw as the solution to racism? Cox in particular articulates the need for a model of counter-education as an antidote to Myrdal's theorization of education as a consensus-producing mechanism and also for calling for consideration of the study's production of whiteness and white subjects. Ending white supremacy, according to Oliver Cox, would involve a form of counter-education that would teach "the white masses to understand and to recognize the ruling class function of racist beliefs and their effect as instruments in the exploitation of the white as well as the black masses."[26]

Yet by limiting their critiques to Myrdal's displacement of the economic origins of racial inequality and racism, these critics also miss the specific ways that Americanization education operates as a rationalizing practice for the professionalization of black subjects toward the goal of middle-class formation, which will enable a process of limited assimilation. Assimilation, as the central goal of the American Creed, is the key to opening U.S. political and economic influence abroad. In Myrdal's narrative of Americanization education, social engineering works as a counterpart, legitimating the incorporations of black subjects toward the goal of producing a mobile workforce to meet the demands of postwar urbanization and industrialization. They did not, however, pick up on how, in Myrdal's narrative, Americanization education works as a racializing mechanism that generates a hierarchical structure as depicted in the model Negro teacher-training school. What is needed for an effective critique of Myrdal is not only a form of counter-education, but also an education that can expose and dismantle the rationalization processes that enable such a hierarchy to develop and also to be maintained.

Americanization education, as the process that Myrdal envisions for the cultural transformation of blacks, serves as the ideological justification and rationalizing practice for such incorporations of black subjects as a mobile professional class into a global imperialist structure. As C. L. R. James suggests, the inferiorization of blacks was inscribed in the structures and workings of state and capital rather than external to the outcome of their histories. More precisely, he suggests that inferiorization as a rationalizing discourse took the specific form of democraticization: To buttress the power of military force, the imperialist had to insist to his own people that they are superior to the exploited races and to the exploited races that they are inferior to his own.[27] James's theorization of blacks as included subjects is important to understanding Myrdal's positioning of Americanization education as a democratic mode of incorporating alien groups into an emergent postwar global order. In Myrdal's model of black professionalization, the inferiorization of blacks could be encased in a concept of "American" cultural education as an inclusionary process of racial uplift. As we will see, Myrdal's model for Negro teacher training offers an apt demonstration of the dynamic of inferiorization as an inclusionary practice: it pathologizes African American culture in a way that also promotes cultural education as the principal mode for incorporating African Americans into the American Creed.

Americanization Education

An American Dilemma registers a shift in attention to what was known popularly and in academic circles as the "Negro problem" in the years during which Myrdal's study was being developed. When Myrdal launched the study in 1938, few white intellectuals were interested in race relations and many of the best scholars were blacks who had been influenced by Marxism. By 1946, however, white liberals were more interested in recognizing civil rights as a critical issue and there were many white intellectuals and journalists writing about blacks.[28] In his concluding chapter, Myrdal offers this assessment of the changing conception of the Negro problem from a "Southern worry" to "national in scope," with "tremendous international implications" (1015). Given the relation to U.S. national progress and international ascension, Myrdal insists that the North could not "compromise" with the white South on the Negro problem. Alternatively, he envisions an education-based model for the resolution of the Negro problem that would simultaneously reform the South's caste system.

Myrdal's proposal to establish a Negro teacher-training college offers a detailed demonstration of his theory that Americanization education, as a process of black professionalization, is the key to separating blacks from the institutions and practices that are hindering their assimilation. In his chapter "The Negro School," he specifically proposes the establishment of a college that would systematize, and presumably raise, the standards for the training of Negro teachers in the South. As a cultural reeducation project that puts the Americanization of the Negro and the socialization of the U.S. South on parallel yet hierarchical tracks, his teacher-training college would transform African Americans from pathologized objects into rational subjects and white southerners from backward slave masters into cooperative state agents under the sponsorship of liberal philanthropists and the auspices of U.S. state and federal management. As a liminal institution between an older system of slavery and emergent forms of imperialism, the Negro teacher training college defines the U.S. South as a training site and enlightened classroom.[29] This model outlines a racial administrative grid that is explicitly hierarchical, but also articulates the necessity of new forms of informal state supervision and overarching federal oversight. As he contends, the establishment of a new model teacher-training college in the U.S. South was a "great service which a farsighted federal policy could undertake in order to equalize educational opportunities for Negroes" (905).

Myrdal's focus on teacher-training programs in "Americanization education" draws from the structure and objectives of established teacher-training programs at the Tuskegee Institute and Hampton Institute that were sponsored by liberal philanthropists, including Andrew Carnegie, John D. Rockefeller, and Julius Rosenwald. In particular, Myrdal's model adapts the management structure of the Jeanes teacher program, in which traveling "rural industrial

supervisors" assist county teachers in organizing their work in domestic science, gardening, and carpentry. Predominantly African American women,
Jeanes teachers were first paid by northern philanthropic funds and eventually by school boards after the formation of the Southern Education Foundation. Working under white male superintendents and school boards, Jeanes
supervisors were likewise supported mostly by northern philanthropists and
controlled by school boards.[30] Myrdal credits Jeanes supervisors with improving southern Negro education but also disparages their obedience to "Southern folkways," implying the need for an objective, modern, and systematic
framework through state and federal participation.[31]

In contrast to U.S. lawmakers, Myrdal saw the South as an economic and
cultural problem rather than a force in national politics.[32] White southerners,
in his narrative, are obstacles to U.S. progress that require new forms of management and federal oversight. In calling for southern reform, Myrdal asks,
"How is it possible to aid without decreasing local responsibility?... *Northern
philanthropy . . . has also had a demoralizing influence on the South*. The South has
become accustomed to taking it for granted that not only rich people in the
North, but also poor church boards, should send money South, thus eternally
repaying 'the responsibility of the North for Reconstruction'" (905; italics in
original). In casting the U.S. South as the setting for the production of a black
professional class, Myrdal attempts to redefine its image from symbol of racial
oppression to an enlightened classroom in the U.S. cultural imagination.

The Negro teacher-training college narrates the professionalization of black
subjects through the systematic transformation of slaveholders into benevolent teachers, thus showcasing the efforts of the United States to incorporate
populations whose absorption also validated the project of American civilization. Presented as a joint northern–southern venture, the training college offered white southerners the opportunity to perform their U.S. citizenship and Anglo-Saxon racial identity by demonstrating their ability to "rule
morally and effectively" over "their savages." So imagined, Myrdal's teacher-
training college employs a tutelary framework that could accommodate elite
African American demands for political participation while putting off issues
of self-determination and economic and material relations and resources. In
Myrdal's model for black professionalization, white southerners are figured
as subjects in need of cultural education, but also as possessing managerial
capacities that could clearly separate them from African Americans. This
hierarchical yet inclusive structure resonates with the U.S. colonial production of racial difference that justified the U.S. elevation of Hispanicized elites
over indigenous "savages" in the Philippines.

Myrdal's blueprint for Americanization education simultaneously articulates a new management structure for U.S. colonial projects in order to project a new image for U.S. postwar hegemony. This critical move can be compared to the U.S. nation-state's attempts to promote teachers, rather than soldiers, as the "true" representatives of U.S. colonialism following President McKinley's 1901 Proclamation of Benevolent Assimilation in the Philippines, which led to the institutionalization of a tutelage-based U.S. policy. Envisioned as a "great army of instruction," the Thomasite educational mission, five hundred white Americans who sailed from the United States to the Philippines on the white USS *Thomas*, began to train Filipino teachers in English in 1901, with the broader mission of preparing Filipinos for their informal U.S. citizenship. This education-centered project was geared toward the production of a common knowledge base between Americans and Filipinos, who were described by the U.S. teachers as "a people who neither know nor understand the underlying principles of our civilization," yet who, "for our mutual happiness and liberty, must be brought into accord with us."[33]

Yet where the Thomasite teachers believed that they were assisting the incorporation of a population that was completely external and alien to American civilization, Myrdal claims that the educational program of the American Creed builds on tendencies and aspirations toward American values and ideals that are already a frame of reference for African Americans and need only to be released by white Americans. Americanization education, as formulated by Myrdal, is a comprehensive process that instructs white Americans on the desirability of extending the creed and that assists blacks in losing their "cultural backwardness" and adopting the dominant "American patterns."[34] The American Creed, he explains, is the principle by which black subjects are prepared to form a mobile class of skilled labor that can meet the demands of wartime industrialization and urbanization and thus be initiated into American rationality and a culture of capitalism that he defines as quintessentially American (94). In Myrdal's teacher-training model, Americanization education forms the basis of a process of racial reform that also articulates a newly configured structure of corporate and state management. His model for black professionalization articulates an inclusive yet explicitly hierarchical structure that takes its form from a racialized division of labor involving regional supervisors, corporate sponsorship, and federal management with an eye toward the expansion of U.S. power and influence abroad. In depicting a black professional class as a long-awaited solution to the Negro problem, Myrdal asserts that, with the proper training in American culture, these professionalized African Americans could have an international impact as representatives of U.S. democracy abroad. Even though the North possessed the political and material resources to bring the South in step through intervention from Congress, the court system, and the executive branch, Myrdal claimed that the new ideological approach of "social engineering" would be a more effective means of reforming the South's caste system (177).

From "Master Organizers of the World" to "Social Engineers"

For Myrdal, social engineering, as a scientific mode of knowledge production that combines the science of "social planning" with an "old American faith in human beings," represents the ideal critical approach for the emergent postwar U.S. nation.[35] With its basis in fact-finding and scientific theories of causal relations, social engineering is instrumental in planning controlled social change as it allows social scientists to standardize the study of "problems" that would be increasingly determined by political decision-making and legislation in the postwar era. Myrdal also emphasizes the capacity of social engineering, through the compilation of sociological data, to "humanize" blacks and to advance their incorporation into the United States' "long gallery of persons" and American Creed. So imagined, social scientists could orient social engineering toward introducing unassimilable groups into a process of rationalization or realizing the universal desire to become "rational and just" (1022).

Myrdal's teacher-training model exemplifies the innovations of social engineering as a new ideological approach to racial reform that will produce a mobile technocracy of color and, in turn, facilitate U.S. international ascension. Even as Myrdal claims to have put aside a polarizing debate over whether Negro education should be liberal or vocational, he directs education and black professionalization toward the creation of an exportable workforce that would pave the way for U.S. global leadership. "What is needed," he claims, "is an education which makes the Negro child adaptable to and moveable in the American culture at large" (906). His conceptualization of a black professionalized class as a specifically mobile one orients educational uplift toward the preparation of a laboring class to meet the new demands of urban industrial capitalism. In describing the urban North's absorption of "untutored and crude Negro immigrants from the South," Myrdal highlights the "heavy burden" of "uneducated masses of Southern born Negroes" on the northern social order and economy in order to advocate for the institutionalization of programs of vocational adult education for black migrants (906).

To advance the white male social scientist as the architect of the U.S. postwar era, Myrdal defines the emergent postwar leadership through its managerial style and capacities. By emphasizing the "white man's burden" in teaching "elements of American culture and also, perhaps, elements of vocational skills" to the masses of African American migrants from the U.S. South, Myrdal articulates the need for social engineering as the social scientific management of an Americanization process that will produce a globally oriented black professional class. Indeed, Myrdal's postwar social scientist, called into being at a key moment in U.S. international ascendancy, has its counterpart in U.S. colonial-era figurations of white Americans as global managers at another key moment of U.S. expansion.[36] In situating the Philippine-American War within the broader cause of "English speaking and Teutonic peoples" at the turn of the nineteenth century, Senator Albert Beveridge of Indiana urged white Americans to manifest their destiny as the "master organizers of the world."[37] Extending the model of white Americans as colonial managers of benevolent uplift, Myrdal's postwar social scientists are interstitial figures that can mediate the interests of the "people," industrial capitalists, and the U.S. government.

According to Myrdal, social scientists could "lead the people to a life based on rational, scientific principles" (xv–xvi). By figuring social engineering, with its basis in rationalism and moralism as the continuation of the Enlightenment project, Myrdal establishes social scientists as the proper guardians of racial reform and U.S. postwar progress.[38] Breaking with the prevailing model of the disinterested intellectual, Myrdal sought to develop a relationship between social science and government policy makers. He envisioned a new figure of the social scientist that would, using planning skills developed during the New Deal and World War II, apply fact-finding and scientific theories in political decision-making to bring about controlled social change. In contrast to Robert Park and other sociologists who believed that sociological studies should be "value neutral" and kept separate from the activities and interests of reformers and government to ensure the scientific status of their investigations, Myrdal argued that social science should take the terms for its studies from the "general beliefs and values of the people."[39] By extending the racialized rationale of U.S. colonial management structures and objectives, he defined social engineering as a process of social transformation encased in a scientific approach.

An American Dilemma needs to be understood, discursively and institutionally, through a discourse of civilization and racial uplift. In this chapter, I have suggested that Myrdal adapts the educational impulses and tutelary framework of U.S. colonial policy to develop Americanization education as a process of black professionalization that would advance U.S. political and economic influence abroad. By bringing into focus the synchronicity between 1940s conceptions of social engineering and nineteenth-century forms of U.S. colonial management, this chapter frames An American Dilemma as a text intended to usher the U.S. nation onto the global stage. To understand U.S. neocolonialism as an extension of the colonial policy of benevolent assimilation, I suggest that we need to look at the ways that postwar models of black professionalization adapt racialized structures of colonial management through a discourse of social engineering.

Breaking with accounts that periodize the influence of An American Dilemma as peaking in the 1940s and ending with the growth of civil rights movements in the early 1960s, as well as those that insist that the study's "enduring power" lies in Myrdal's moral challenge to Americans, I suggest instead that the sociological study's legacy can be found in its expansion of an inclusionary process that operates through the inferiorization of African American knowledge production on race as well as the production of a professionalized class of color as a globally exportable body of labor.

To consider a specific historical moment and cultural instance of the institutionalization of such an inclusionary discourse, the chapter offers an exemplary reading of Myrdal's proposal for a Negro teacher-training college in the U.S. South, focusing on the conditions under which Americanization education became a compelling way to present black professionalization as a means of carrying out southern reform, resolving the Negro problem, and rationalizing new forms of federal oversight and state supervision. This notion that education will solve racial inequality has become a key assumption of neoliberal discourse, as it also assists assumptions that racism is the outcome of working-class ignorance and can be eliminated by expanding the middle class and standardizing middle-class perspectives.

As chapters 3 and 4 show, Filipino and Asian Pacific American writers specifically took up sociology's theorization of African Americans and Asian Americans as included subjects rather than only as excluded subjects in the national polity. By rearticulating the discontinuities in sociology's inclusionary address as self-authorizing discourses, these writers attempt to locate themselves in the emerging postwar global order.

3.

Training for the American Century

Professional Filipinos in Carlos Bulosan's America Is in the Heart

In his influential 1941 editorial "The American Century," Henry R. Luce, the publisher of *Life* and *Time*, placed a corps of "engineers, scientists, doctors, movie men, makers of entertainment, developers of airlines, builders of roads, teachers, educators" at the heart of his vision of the twentieth century as a period of U.S. global dominance.[1] Describing the United States as the "training center of the skillful servants of mankind," Luce suggested that an American-dominated world order—and, by extension, postwar democracy and liberty for all nations—could be secured through the development, reproduction, and dissemination of American expertise (171). By portraying the flow of skilled workers as a "humanitarian army of Americans," Luce cast the United States as "the Good Samaritan" and specified the expansion of experts and knowledge practices in the postwar world as its central task (170).

"The American Century" has been understood primarily as an idealistic vision of U.S. hegemony. Frequently analyzed as a governing theory in national history, scholars have noted how it spurred the cultural identity and powerful self-image of the post–World War II United States as the leader of a new and benevolent global order. But what Luce specifically describes is the emergence of a professional class as a historical formation at a critical moment of U.S. ascendancy. At a time of increasing demand in the United States for "informal" labor performed by a racialized workforce of noncitizens, particularly Filipinos and Mexicans, he cast a professional corps as the principal protagonists in a narrative of U.S. postwar progress. As he saw it, an emergent technocracy could strengthen and revise a cultural link between the United States and Europe by establishing the United States as "the sanctuary of the ideals of civilization" and, with the decline of European nations, the rightful heir of Western civilization (171).

Yet Luce's definition of postwar professionals as celebrated American citizens and of homegrown expertise as patriotic work resonated deeply with Filipino American writers. In defining knowledge production as the quintessential American activity of the post–World War II era, Luce inadvertently gave Filipinos, as U.S. colonial subjects, a purchase on U.S. identity. If the mobile, American-style education of a professional class was to be the distinguishing feature of the postwar era, then it presented the distinct possibility of recognizing the impact of benevolent assimilation, the colonial policy of tutelage for Filipinos, and constructing Filipinos and Filipino Americans as experts on processes of Americanization.[2]

The question of what style of governance the United States should employ in the Philippines continued to be a topic of intense debate in the years following the U.S. annexation of the Philippines in 1899. The specter of Filipinos was largely believed to have receded from public view in the years afterward and until the mid-1920s, with the emergence of what was popularly known as the "Filipino race problem" on the West Coast of the United States. As Oscar Campomanes notes, "All talk of further colonization of the world's vast spaces would effectively cease (and the Philippine Question itself falls out of the picture) after 1904, and the U.S. presumably begins to make another customary retreat to 'isolationism' and the reconfiguration of its own markets (the largest in the world) to resolve U.S. capitalism's endemic crises."[3] Using Luce's focus on U.S.-trained professionals to recover a history of benevolent assimilation in the Philippines and for Filipino Americans was particularly significant for Filipino writers, as it also provided a way to bring into view the question of U.S. imperialism and to unsettle the notion that the United States had adopted an ideology of isolationism in the early twentieth century.

Though substantially absent from the discourse on Filipino migration before World War II, professional Filipinos figured centrally in texts by Filipino writers in the United States during the 1940s and 1950s. Why did professionals become the key fact of Filipino visibility for Filipino American writers at this particular historical moment? By looking closely at Carlos Bulosan's well-known autobiography *America Is in the Heart* (1946), I will consider the conditions of possibility under which Filipino professionals became an acceptable, even compelling way to imagine Filipino migration and agency in the postwar United States. This representational shift was neither a coincidence nor solely a response to changes within Filipino migration itself. Although earlier waves of Filipino migration included *pensionados*, students who were studying in the United States, the 14,000 Filipinos who traveled to the United States between 1920 and 1929 were primarily migrant laborers working in agriculture in California and the Pacific Northwest and in the salmon canneries of Alaska. The importation of Filipinos was largely a result of the 1924 Immigration Act, which banned Japanese immigration, leading the agricultural industry to replace Japanese laborers with Filipinos and Mexicans.[4] To explain why Filipino writers, including Bulosan, Bienvenido Santos, and F. Sionil José, turned to professional Filipinos in their works during the 1940s and 1950s, I propose that we consider this question within the context of Luce's contemporaneous focus on an emergent technocracy as a description of postwar global realignment.

This chapter suggests that their critical focus on professional Filipinos tells an important story about knowledge production at the moment in which postwar U.S. ascendancy was being conceptualized by a specific class of professional experts that included Luce and sociologists of race. Situating Bulosan's struggling writer, Santos's traveling lecturer ("Scent of Apples") and stranded Washington bureaucrats ("Brown Coterie"), and José's disenchanted advertising executive ("The Light Bringer") and government agency men ("The God Stealer") in relation to narratives of U.S. ascendancy complicates our understandings of "The American Century" by placing it in the same discursive universe as U.S. colonialism and neocolonialism in the Philippines and for Filipino Americans. At the same time, this interpretive move offers us a more nuanced view of Filipino writers as knowledge producers who selectively engaged, invoked, and contested historic and representational conventions in an emergent neocolonial discourse of which they were part.

Of the works that focus on professional Filipinos, Bulosan's text specifically traces the emergence of a figure defined by the capacity to gather, organize, generate, and disseminate knowledge that could compete with the dominant and readily available representations of Filipinos (as brown monkeys, little brown brothers, sexualized natives, model servants). *America Is in the Heart* is also the best-known Filipino American text and circulates widely in academic and community contexts. Since its recovery by Asian American writers and multiculturalism of the early 1970s, Bulosan's book has been taught in Asian American studies and U.S. literature and history courses, adapted for performances by Filipino community theater groups, and excerpted in labor union publications. Frequently described as a documentary history of

Filipinos in the United States, *America Is in the Heart* is a story about Filipino migrant workers in the Philippines and on the West Coast of the United States from the 1920s through the early 1940s. Narrated from the perspective of Carlos, Bulosan's autobiographical protagonist, the book chronicles the encounters of poor Filipinos with a quasi-feudal system of Philippine land ownership, exploitative labor contractors, and a growing anti-Filipino movement in the racially segregated United States. Read as a narrative of Filipino identity formation, *America Is in the Heart* dramatizes the efforts of the *manongs*, Filipino male laborers who traveled to the United States in the early part of the twentieth century to form a labor movement and develop proletarian consciousness.[5]

But, as I argue below, Bulosan's text seems more interested in fleshing out the figure of a professional Filipino knowledge producer. Rather than treating this focus as an anomaly or aberration, I propose that it provided a way for him to investigate the implications of benevolent assimilation for Filipinos in the United States, particularly the question of Filipino agency. Indeed, Luce's description of the United States as the "training center" for the postwar global order offered a particularly rich figure for Bulosan to evoke a colonial history of Filipino contact with training processes of Americanization and to open up its postwar implications. In taking up Luce's vision of a postwar era dominated by a professional class, Bulosan relied upon Luce's fundamentally elitist logic but also transformed it into a critique of a liberal epistemology that narrates U.S. postwar dominance as a progressive developmental narrative through the incorporation and relational racialization of U.S. colonized subjects.

Even as he referenced Luce's alignment of an emergent technocracy with U.S. postwar hegemony, Bulosan did not figure Filipino professionals as the appropriate or authentic representatives of postwar Filipino identity or as a way to champion an elite class as an alternative to the conventional emphasis on Filipino working classes. Instead, his focus on a professional Filipino migrant subject served as an entry point for questioning the narrative of postwar U.S. ascendancy imposed in Luce's "American Century." Investigating the impact of Bulosan's chosen focus on Filipino professionals enables us to examine the emergence of a liberal epistemology that narrated post–World War II U.S. dominance as a progressive developmental narrative rather than a transition between U.S. colonialism and neocolonialism.

To adapt Luce's focus on American experts and knowledge practices in his vision of U.S. preeminence, Bulosan had to consider how the colonial policy of benevolent assimilation envisioned a narrative of Filipino tutelage.

In contrast to immigrant narratives that feature ethnic subjects striving to make it in America, benevolent assimilation imposed a narrative of progress that featured liberal white Americans as the main protagonists. To consider the novelties and discontinuities of this narrative, Bulosan refigured benevolent assimilation as an authorizing discourse rather than a civilizing process for Filipinos in the Philippines and Filipino Americans. He could then suggest that the American education of Filipinos under benevolent assimilation exemplified Luce's vision of mobile American expertise.

Producing Benevolent Supremacy/Remembering Benevolent Assimilation

Bulosan's text links the reformist impulses of benevolent assimilation to those found in Luce's "American Century," illuminating the intersection between U.S. colonialism and postwar expansion. In narrating the rise of postwar U.S. world power as an elaboration of the U.S. colonial policy of benevolent assimilation, Bulosan attempted to intervene in a discourse of what Charles Hilliard termed "benevolent supremacy." Hilliard, in *The Cross, the Sword, and the Dollar*, used benevolent supremacy to describe U.S. global expansion as a positive postwar political doctrine and to promote conceptions of the United States as a benevolent, anti-imperial power.[6] What was critical to the discourse of benevolent supremacy was the idea that the extension of U.S. global influence was dramatically different from that of European empires, which paved the way for the self-representation of the United States as an anti-imperial nation. As William Appleman Williams observed in 1959, traditional conceptions of an anti-imperialist America enabled the United States to acknowledge having once had an empire while also legitimating its claim to having given it away.[7]

As Melani McAlister observes, benevolent supremacy offered a multitude of possibilities for the self-representation of the ascendance of U.S. international power to Americans: "The diverse and overlapping sites for the production of 'benevolent supremacy' were precisely what gave the discourse its richness and flexibility—and its salience. In the statements of foreign policy officials, in popular culture, newspaper and magazine articles, and in the highly visible staging of U.S. foreign policy, the discourse was powerful precisely because it was multifaceted and variously located."[8] Filipino writers such as Bulosan could thus engage a discourse of benevolent supremacy to examine forms of U.S. expansion that elaborated on benevolent assimilation and were not limited to direct military or political action.

The significance of recovering and evaluating benevolent assimilation in the early 1940s was profound, particularly in the wake of the Hare-Hawes-Cutting Act of 1932 and the Tydings-McDuffie Act of 1934, which established a Philippine commonwealth and ten-year transition period to independence. The gradualist plan for Philippine independence outlined in the Tydings-McDuffie Act sought to define the Philippine commonwealth as a separate country and limited the Philippine immigration quota to fifty per year. Even as the Immigration Act of 1924 set one hundred as the maximum annual immigration quota from other countries, the U.S. tutelage of Filipinos under benevolent assimilation did not secure equal treatment, but instead classed them only slightly above fully excluded Oriental groups, such as Chinese, Japanese, and Koreans.[9] Yet the trajectory for Philippine independence was disrupted by the Japanese occupation of the Philippines from 1941 to 1944, which ejected U.S. troops, sent the commonwealth government into exile, and raised the question of the postwar status of the Philippines.

In elaborating the narrative of progress for Filipino uplift and reform implied by the policy of benevolent assimilation, the notion of Philippine independence under commonwealth status reproduced features of the colonial relationship. One of the central assumptions of the U.S. colonial project in the Philippines was that Filipinos were comprised of uncivilized tribes and thus incapable of self-government. Outlining the United States' "commitment" to individual rather than national freedom in the Philippines in 1899, President McKinley stated, "We come not as invaders or conquerors, but as friends, to protect the natives in their homes, in their employments, and in their personal and religious rights. . . . The mission of the United States is one of benevolent assimilation."[10] Benevolent assimilation specifically outlined a period in which Filipinos in the Philippines and the United States were to be the objects of U.S. uplift. In extending the dubious promise of civilization to Filipinos and Filipino Americans, benevolent assimilation also held out to liberal white Americans, as Vicente Rafael observes, "the promise of fathering, as it were, a 'civilized people' capable in time of asserting its own character."[11] As an insular rather than immigration policy, benevolent assimilation imposed a civilizing process for Filipinos in the Philippines and the United States as objects who would eventually, through the benevolent intervention and example of liberal white Americans, become Americanized and self-determined subjects, but not U.S. citizens.

By taking up the narrative of U.S. progress implied by benevolent supremacy, Filipinos could point to the ironies of benevolent assimilation, particularly surrounding the status of Filipinos as colonial subjects whose uplift was a defining feature of U.S. imperiality.[12] Filipino farm workers used this strategy to demand social equality and equal wages in the United States during the 1920s. Responding to charges that cheap Filipino workers posed a threat to white labor, Filipinos attempted to mitigate anti-Filipino sentiment by insisting on equal wages. In their demands to California asparagus growers, Filipino workers drew directly from the rhetoric of benevolent assimilation: "Filipino workers intended and always do intend to uphold and EMULATE the STANDARD OF AMERICAN WAGES."[13] For Filipino writers, bringing into view Filipino migration to the metropole made it possible to examine the contradictions of the status of Filipinos under the policy of benevolent assimilation, which drew upon notions of destiny and duty as justifications for the colonization of the Philippines. As colonial subjects, Filipinos were neither U.S. citizens nor aliens, but were instead classified as U.S. nationals. Even as they owed their allegiance to the United States, they were not entitled to the same rights as citizens, such as the right to representation and trial by jury.

Brown Bodies of Discourse

In *America Is in the Heart*, Bulosan constructs a richly textured web of knowledge produced about Filipinos in the Philippines and the United States. Where and when, he asks, do Filipinos enter the field of representation?[14] To address this epistemological question, Bulosan suggests that Filipino subject formations are intertwined with the ethnographic and colonial processes by which knowledge about Filipinos is produced. In depicting incidents in which Filipinos are the objects of ethnographic and colonial discourses, he also situates Carlos as a self-reflexive interpreter and analyst of each episode.

Recounting an incident in which an American female tourist offers Carlos money to undress before her camera, Bulosan calls attention to his understanding of what Western tourists interpret and value as Filipino:

> What interested the tourists most were the naked Igorot women and their children. Sometimes they took pictures of the old men with G-strings. They were not interested in Christian Filipinos like me. They seemed to take a particular delight in photographing young Igorot girls with large breasts and robust mountain men whose genitals were nearly exposed, their G-strings bulging large and alive.[15]

This scene, and indeed Bulosan's book, is representative of a major shift in conceptions of Filipino agency in the midcentury United States. In depicting the production of Filipinos as ethnographic objects, Bulosan points to the specific demand by Western tourists for sexualized representations of racialized

Filipino natives and also raises questions of Filipino self-representation and economic survival. But the most compelling part of his description is the way in which it calls attention to his own capacity for evaluating how these knowledge practices call into being representations of racialized sexual otherness and label them as Filipino. He thus defines the knowing subject as a Christianized Filipino, implying that this subject emerges through his reenactment of colonial knowledge practices and in contrast to the spectacularized Filipino natives.

When Miss Mary Strandon, a white American librarian, reprimands Carlos for attempting to construct himself as a native object for tourist photographs, she provides him with what she sees as a better alternative: becoming an efficient domestic helper. As "Little Brown Brother," Carlos learns to feel ashamed of trying to objectify himself as a native and attempts to be the ideal colonial subject, only to discover the limitations implicit in this notion of mimetic consciousness.[16] While living with Miss Strandon, he does the cooking and cleaning according to her standards and example, gets a job in a library, and undergoes an epiphany as a result of his new contact with books. For Carlos, the "new world" that is opened to him leads to acts of memory and comparison rather than humanist enlightenment. His job at the library does not lift him out of the category of "Little Brown Brother," but instead provides him with the "opportunity" to compare the mansions of wealthy library patrons with his family's grass hut. Though he sees himself as fortunate for finding work in a library and having access to books, he finds that the subject position of "Little Brown Brother" does not enfranchise him in an American meritocracy, but instead provides a way for him to consider how such entitlements are specifically racialized. Later in life he reads about how Richard Wright was refused books by his local library and claims that it enables him to take an analytical perspective on his present situation. Carlos represents this change of consciousness as a precursor to his production of a book on American life, suggesting that this turn marks his departure from the path of uplift on which Miss Strandon had placed him. For Bulosan, becoming a writer is a process that takes place by learning to negotiate the subject positions of "native" and "Little Brown Brother." To contrast Carlos's transformation with the liberal narrative of progress implied by benevolent assimilation, Bulosan closes the episode by offering us a view of Carlos as a knowledge producer and library donor rather than an object and beneficiary. Recalling his visit to Strandon's Iowa hometown, Carlos, now the confident narrator, sums up his critical encounter with the civilizing process that she represents: "I wrote her name on a copy of my first book and donated it to the local library. I think she would have been happy to know that I would someday write a book about her country (71)."

Becoming an Expert among Others

Of the many discursive connections that Bulosan establishes in relation to these processes, those that were sociological were particularly important. Considering sociological knowledge production and Bulosan's text as part of the same mid-twentieth-century U.S. discursive universe illuminates a broad development in the ideological import of sociological studies of race, promoting a clearer view of how and why, at this historical moment, fictional writings on communities of color were increasingly engineered through, and often confused with, sociological representations. To question the ways in which writings by people of color are often read as sociology, or as texts that transparently reflect the "truth" of racialized experience, I situate sociology as an ideologically and historically constituted discourse. This move seems especially critical when we consider that by 1940, the discipline of sociology had become the privileged discourse on race and its implications for U.S. national progress.

The rise of sociology as the official discourse on race helped to situate the sociologist of race at the center of national politics. Robert E. Park and the Chicago School sociologists who were studying communities of color as racial problems (for example, the Negro problem and the Oriental problem) were increasingly regarded as the dominant authorities on race relations and the "architects" of the nation's future. As part of this context and also in response to the increase in Filipino migration following the ban on Oriental immigration mandated in the 1924 Immigration Act, Park's former student, Emory Bogardus, whose own students included many Filipinos, directed numerous studies of the "Filipino race problem" at the University of Southern California during the 1930s.[17] Despite this phenomenon, however, the relationship between sociological studies of the Filipino problem and Bulosan's text is largely assumed to have been one of factual, rather than ideological and institutional, influence.

Cultural historians have traced the emergence of a Filipino problem to the late 1920s, with the eruptions of racial violence against Filipino laborers in California and the Pacific Northwest. During this time, sociological studies that focused on the Filipino race problem shaped academic and popular thought about Filipinos, but also shaped the development of sociology's analytical conventions and self-representation as a rising profession. When sociologists sought to determine Filipino racial identity, they found that their studies of Filipinos were structured by comparisons and discussions of intersections. In his studies on the Filipino problem and the color line in California, Donald Elliott Anthony asked questions about the similarities and differences between Filipinos and Orientals. By investigating how comparisons and intersections with other groups that had been defined as problems gave meaning to the racialized category of "Filipino," he concluded that the color line applied to Filipinos as well as Orientals.[18]

To understand how Filipinos were different from Orientals or how Filipinos were and were not American, Anthony had to consider the subjective thought and self-understanding of Filipinos as valuable scientific data. In this way, sociological research on the Filipino problem gave discursive and institutional value to the notion of Filipino subjectivity. The emphasis that sociologists placed on subjectivity, however, did not mean that they did not continue to use biologically based assumptions in their arguments on Filipino racialization. According to Anthony, the main difference between the Filipino problem and the Oriental problem could be traced to the "attitude of the Filipino."[19] In arguing that Filipinos, in contrast to Orientals, did not see themselves as naturally subordinate, and in fact resented being classed with Orientals, Anthony took into account the colonial status of the Philippines and the education-oriented policy of benevolent assimilation, but also drew conclusions based on assumptions about the nature of Filipinos.

Research on the Filipino problem provided an important staging ground for sociologists of race to consolidate their explanatory authority and define their expertise as uniquely American. In his 1932 chapter "What Race Are Filipinos?" Emory Bogardus describes Filipinos as an "admixture almost as mixed as Americans in the United States."[20] Using language that reinforces both a proprietary relation to Filipinos and a pluralist national identity, Bogardus writes: "What race are Filipinos? Not one yet, but one in the making. What shall we label them racially, if they must be labeled? The answer depends in part on what racial classification we use."[21] Defining Filipino racial identity as a work in progress, Bogardus placed Filipino racial identity under the stewardship of white American experts. In doing so, he elaborated the narrative of Filipino uplift toward a white American ideal implied by the policy of benevolent assimilation, but defined it as part of a scientific and objective process. Rather than exercising power over these subjects, sociologists of race emerge from these discursive practices as intelligently and objec-tively giving order and life to the Filipino.

We can thus see Bulosan's engagement with racialized sexual stereotypes as part of a larger context involving a series of legislative acts that positioned sociological knowledge production as a lever for securing the U.S.-state pro-tection of white racial identity. Such links between academic scientific studies of Filipinos and the creation of racist laws are made clear in Carlos's account of Filipino racialization: "Anthropologists and other experts maintained that Filipinos are not Mongolians, but members of the Malayan race. It was then a simple thing for the state legislature to pass a law forbidding mar-riage between members of the Malayan and Caucasian races (143)."[22] Filipino racial identity, as Bulosan suggests, is a product of discriminatory legislation that draws upon scientific studies of the Filipino problem. Sociological stud-ies of the Filipino problem may thus be seen as part of a long prehistory of Filipino American literature.

To become a knowledge producer, Bulosan had to adapt a sanctioned dis-course that would enable him to compete with scientific experts who were studying the Filipino problem. He turns to scientific language to convey rising anti-Filipino sentiment, defining it as a "condition" that structures and haunts the lives of Filipinos in the United States. Rather than presenting his encoun-ters with racist violence in purely personal terms, Bulosan borrows scientific terms and narratives to situate a series of racist incidents in which he is the object within a larger context and gives them collective meaning. In taking up the form of a generic sociological narrative, Bulosan figures himself as both an unenlightened subject who does not understand the "vast social implications of the discrimination against Filipinos" as well as an analyst who develops the perspective to interpret events and to retrospectively highlight their impor-tance (143). Instead of relating a liberal humanist epiphany, Carlos's story focuses on how he adopted a specific set of knowledge practices that enable him to analyze a situation in which he had before been only the object.

The historic and material pressures specific to *America Is in the Heart* cen-ter on objectification and racialization as mutually constitutive processes in U.S. history. To describe Carlos's shift from object to subject, Bulosan takes up a narrative implied by the sociological concept of *social process*, which Bogardus defined as a description of social changes and the effects of these changes on the attitudes and values on all the people involved. The sci-entific value of this process for the study of social problems, he explains, is not located in the description itself, but rather in its significance in "human terms."[23] The concept of social process thus placed a premium on the representation of subjectivity. Modern sociology, as envisioned by Bogardus, could thus breathe new life into the raw material of statistical data.

The elevated status that sociologists of race gave to notions of self-understanding served to define sociology as a humane and forward-looking field and also distinguished it from other academic disciplines. Park specifically separated the objectives and work of sociologists from those of historians, sociologists, and statisticians. Sociologists, according to Park, did not concern themselves with facts. Gathering facts, he asserts, was the work of the historian, whereas enumerating and analyzing facts were tasks undertaken by the statistician. Following Park's formulation, sociology could then be seen as "interested in the *meanings* of facts to the persons involved, hence in the study of attitudes and how they change."[24] The ideal perspective, in this sense, was a combination of empathy and objectivity that would, in turn, enable an understanding of the development of attitudes and values within a broad social context.

Bulosan's text develops the novelties and discontinuities of sociological studies of race, offering a remix of racialized gendered stereotypes, legal cases, and interactions between Filipino migrant laborers. In doing so, he takes to heart sociology's standard of combining empathy and objectivity. This perspective made it not only possible to include firsthand accounts by Filipinos, but such inclusions actually made the project more valuable and interesting from a sociological perspective. It thus offered the possibility of authorizing Bulosan as an expert knower. Whereas sociologists such as Bogardus produced knowledge on the racial classification of Filipinos and promoted sociology as a specific professional field and an "American" social science, Filipino writers such as Bulosan focused on Filipino professionals as experts on Americanization.

Significantly, Bulosan's interest in the conditions under which knowledge about Filipinos is produced suggests a closer relationship with discourses of sociology than labor history. While works on Filipino and Mexican agricultural labor by historians such as Carey McWilliams, including *Brothers under the Skin* (1943) and *Factories in the Field* (1939), might appear to be the more obvious discursive connection, I suggest that investigating the intersections between Bulosan's text and sociological studies of race can tell us more about why Bulosan consistently foregrounds processes of knowledge production. Whereas labor history sought to illuminate the material and ideological factors that shaped broad dynamics of labor relations and capital, sociology was concerned with the intertwined processes of knowledge production and subject formation. Although both sociological studies of race and labor histories that focused on Filipino agricultural laborers have historically contributed to and legitimated racial stereotypes of Filipinos, sociological studies of race opened compelling possibilities for Filipino self-representation.

That New Professional Perspective

By 1940, the field of sociology had become the authoritative discourse on race in the United States, but it had also expanded its professional presence. As a privileged expert on race relations and the nation's future, the academic sociologist of race offered a powerful model of a professional knowledge producer. Bogardus, the Chicago School sociologist who studied the Filipino problem in California, was also a renowned institution builder, famous for his contributions to professionalizing the discipline of sociology. Around the same time that he developed his studies of Filipinos, Bogardus systematized sociological research methods and spearheaded the production of sociology textbooks, journals, and professional associations. His seminal concept of *social distance*, defined as the "difference in sympathetic understanding that exists between persons, or groups, or between a person and a group," was particularly important in giving value to the subjective thoughts and ideas of people of color.[25] Elaborating on Park's view of sociology as a combination of empathy and objectivity, Bogardus developed a system for measuring changes in attitudes toward different races, classes, and nationalities. As an analytic convention and scientific tool, Bogardus's system gave value to the subjectivities of marginalized groups, even as such self-expressions were highly mediated by the sociological contexts, rhetoric, and categories of experience.

Sociology produced a discourse around Filipinos that included subjectivity, providing Bulosan with a set of meanings for his environment and a sense of agency via the ability to interpret and understand situations in which he had been only the confused object. Bulosan's text reflects Carlos's transition from object to developing agent as a change that emerges through reading books. In describing his turn to books during his hospitalization for tuberculosis, Bulosan foregrounds the details of his studies, thematizing his complex and conflicted location in his description of his reaction to each text. As he puts it, reading books develops his "spiritual kinship with other men who had pondered over the miseries of their countries" (246). Reading books about global revolutionary struggles thus provides a way for him to connect to a professional class of writers of different nations and historical moments. This episode thus operates as a working bibliography, illuminating the specific conditions under which Carlos comes to view himself as a reader and critic, assessing the literary value of each text and offering detailed descriptions of their examples as writers. The inspiration that Carlos finds, for example, in Maxim Gorky's "lowly birth, his wanderings in the vast Russian land, his sufferings and the nameless people who suffered for him" expresses his interest in proletarian struggles but also indicates an interest in the rise of a particular kind of migrant writer, one from a poor family and with little formal education (246). Indeed, Carlos's fascination with Gorky also separates him from anti-Stalinist intellectuals in the United States who condemned Gorky for "selling out." In Bulosan's text, then, books do not represent a desire to escape from reality, but instead enable Carlos to envision himself as part of a professional class of writers.

Carlos emerges as an analyst and knowledge producer called into being at a specific historical moment. As his account suggests, claiming Gorky also helped to align him with American writers that include Hart Crane and John Fante, whose works also took up themes of belonging, uprootedness, and migrant life. Rather than focusing on individual works or national traditions, Carlos envisions a global network of writers, including Filipino writer Manuel Arguilla, who focus on working classes and revolutionary struggles:

> While Federico García Lorca was writing passionately about the folklore of the peasants in Granada, Nicolás Guillén was changing verses of social equality for the Negro people in Puerto Rico. While André Malraux was dramatizing the heroism of the Chinese Communists, a Filipino, Manuel E. Arguilla, was writing of the peasantry on the island of Luzon. (246)

Claiming that the significance of their works goes beyond national contexts and forms of belonging, Carlos situates himself as part of a politicized professional network and literary history.

David Lloyd, in a reading of Immanuel Kant's *Critique of Judgment*, describes a process of human subject formation in which the senses move from recognition of local or individual matter and extend to universalist forms, or to a civic sense. This recognition of universalist forms, Lloyd contends, is possible only through the assumption of a position of disinterested subjecthood, since competing forms of identification would have to be subordinated for such an interpellation to take place. According to Lloyd, the process of identification with universalist forms represents a formalization of the subject or the hegemonic imposition of a universalist form upon heterogeneous elements.[26] In *America Is in the Heart*, however, the process of identification with concepts of enlightenment subjectivity and development is used as a rhetorical strategy that inspires critiques of their universalist assumptions. The inversion of such "formalizations of the subject" enables the production of subjectivity that is not in service to the nation-state; in the novel, the narrator extends his interpretation of various literary texts to identify with the political and aesthetic struggles of other writers, which enables the production of an oppositional, proletarian, and Filipino American subjectivity. In contrast to Lloyd's view of subject formation, the narrator's identification with other writers and development of aesthetic judgment does not represent what Lloyd terms an "ethical end of humanity," but rather the beginning of an understanding of his position in relation to other political and aesthetic debates.[27]

Bulosan's act of remembering is, in one sense, his solution to his personal dilemma. His literary studies lead him to rethink notions of temporality and history in a way that makes it possible to remember that Filipinos have been forgotten and why it is important to understand why this has been the case. Crediting his study of world folklore as the catalyst for his discovery of the Philippine national hero Jose Rizal, an anticolonial Filipino writer who was executed by Spanish authorities, Bulosan focuses on his lack of understanding: "Why I had forgotten him until now, I did not know" (260). Again, his recovery of Rizal, a Filipino nationalist, disinters the legacies of Spanish colonialism, posing as a personal memory that enables the return of an official history of Filipino resistance to colonization.

Developing the persona of an analyst also prepares Carlos to interpret his immediate surroundings from what he sees as the proper perspective. He foregrounds the warrant for studying anti-Filipino hostility in a way that also presupposes that he has a broader point of view than those of the subjects he studies, as well as a richer background to reflect upon the data and an appropriate plan for analyzing it. Relating his arrival in San Diego, Carlos remarks that he is part of a "condition" of white antagonism toward Filipinos that he attributes to a hatred of Filipino intermarriage with whites. Although he connects this racial hostility to his inability to get a job and to the frequent beatings he receives from restaurant and hotel proprietors, he initially blames "bad" Filipinos as the cause for his treatment. Drawing on the purportedly objective language of social science, Carlos, now the confident narrator, offers an analysis of his initial response: "This misconception was generated by a confused personal reaction to dynamic social forces" (143). Even as he claims that his quest for truth led him to develop a fresh perspective, he also connects this "proper" perspective to scientific language and narratives. In telling this story, Bulosan does not follow the generic outline of a classic tale of personal growth and enlightenment. Rather than focusing on Carlos's journey from myopia to 20/20 vision or aligning the climax of the episode with Carlos's liberation or integration within the dominant social order, Bulosan takes up the conventions of the enlightenment narrative, focusing on Carlos's adoption of a scientific perspective and presenting this shift as the critical turning point of the episode.

Adapting the explanatory authority of sociologists of race provides Bulosan with a way to generate counternarratives to sociological studies of Filipinos. Whereas sociologists linked the Filipino race problem to the all-male composition of the Filipino workforce and the deviation of Filipino community formations from a heterosexual family norm, Bulosan depicts a Filipino male workforce as emerging out of historical conditions. In contrast to the absence of family and stable community emphasized in sociological representations of Filipinos, his text points to Filipino efforts to develop labor and literary networks. While sociological studies depicted Filipino homosocial communities as aberrations to an American pattern of assimilation, Bulosan depicts them as historical formations that emerge in response to colonial policy, anti-Filipino violence, and racial segregation. In describing the development of a Filipino network, he offers an alternative to sociological accounts of Filipino community formations and indicates the need for new analytical approaches.

Revising a Rural Migrant Subject

The appearance of Bulosan's figure of the Filipino writer is even more interesting when read as part of a wider discourse on rural migrants. For Bulosan, the representation of the rural migrant subject was a profoundly formative discourse that served to interpellate the citizens of a nation that was largely believed to have adopted an isolationist politics and that had supposedly turned inward to focus on domestic reforms such as employment, government, and social welfare. The fascination of U.S. audiences with the figure of the rural migrant has been primarily traced by cultural historians to 1930s New Deal social programs. As Mae Ngai observes, projecting a "docile, white, pathetically poor, and passive image" to the American public enabled federal agencies to consolidate an image of the U.S. government as humane, committed to social welfare, and concerned about migrants (rather than only settled communities) at the same time that race riots and labor conflicts intensified in California and the Pacific Northwest.[28] To elaborate on Ngai's argument, I would add that the story of the Dust Bowl migrant worker was powerful because it could be compelling to U.S. audiences on a national scale rather than a regional one. Government attention to the plight of the white rural migrant increasingly became accepted as a sign of U.S. liberalism and democracy. Not only did public interest in the figure of the Dust Bowl migrant bring about a narrative that featured the uplift of a rural migrant through the intervention of state programs, but it was also instrumental in shaping conceptions of the United States as a nation of elite white reformers.

Here I wish to return to Luce's arguments regarding a professional class, as the notion of a reform-oriented citizen–subject is central to his concept of "The American Century." If Luce retained the reformist emphasis of the New Deal, then he also reoriented it toward postwar global realignment rather than an internal agenda.[29] U.S. postwar expansion could thus be scripted as an expanded liberal narrative that featured American professionals, rather than progressive white Americans, as benevolent global agents.

Bulosan drew upon Luce's notion of a reform-oriented professional for his figure of a Filipino writer, but portrayed its emergence as a historical formation. His interest in the possibilities that 1930s rural migrant discourse offers for conceptualizing a Filipino writer seems less unusual if we consider the dissonance that is invoked by his juxtaposition of Carlos and John Custer, a "poor American boy" (247). This dissonance may be traced to the way in which popular conceptions of New Deal programs as progressive, national programs contribute to the exclusion of "informal" labor from national social welfare programs as well as the dominant discourse on rural migrants. Drawing a distressing parallel between Custer's convalescence in the main hospital and Carlos's lodging near the hospital jail, Bulosan announced to his readers the differently racialized perceptions and privileges accorded to them. As if further clarification were required, this episode also invokes racialized perceptions of Filipino men as criminals and libidinous threats to white women to underscore the different subject positions of Carlos and Custer. Rather than delivering a scene of fraternal bonding, this brief exchange between Carlos and John Custer demonstrates Bulosan's close engagement with the prevailing U.S. cultural and political discourse on rural migrants during the 1930s and adapts it to refer to Filipinos.[30]

During the 1930s, the Farm Security Administration and other government agencies developed key national and social welfare programs for rural migrants, but did not include noncitizens, nationals, and contract workers as part of this category. Mexicans and Filipinos, as foundational groups of the agricultural workforce that were also deeply invested in raising standards of agricultural labor, were not factored into the Farm Security Administration's

labor camp experiments that were geared toward providing minimum facilities for health, safety, living, and education to migratory workers. Furthermore, racial segregation practices and migrant life helped to ensure that
white Dust Bowl migrants would benefit from these experiments, as Mexicans generally lived in rural *colonias* and Filipinos in ethnic labor camps.[31]
For Filipinos and Mexicans, the supposedly universal notion of uplift through
labor and concept of the migrant worker that such programs call into being
were formulated around standards and norms that were not only impossible
to conform to, but that contributed to their "private" disenfranchisement,
locating them outside of mainstream discussions of labor and social reform at
the moment of U.S. ascendancy.

Reading *America Is in the Heart* in the context of 1930s rural migrant discourse makes Bulosan's appropriation of Custer's voice especially intriguing.
In describing how Carlos comes to write a letter to Custer's mother in Arkan-
sas, Bulosan does not show us the text of the letter, but instead foregrounds
how assuming Custer's position enables him to relate his personal narrative
and portray it as American: "I was no longer writing about this lonely sick
boy, but about myself and my friends in America. I told her about the lean,
the lonely and miserable years. I mentioned places and names. I was not writing to an unknown mother any more. I was writing to my own mother plow-
ing in the muddy fields of Mangusmana: it was the one letter I should have
written before. I was telling her about America" (247). The combination of
assuming the position of the Dust Bowl migrant and reimagining his relationship with a white woman are the conditions that enable the release of
Carlos's personal narrative about Filipinos in the United States.

Bulosan accordingly defines Americanization as a process applicable to
colonized subjects and white Americans. Years later, Custer writes a letter to
Carlos and casts his acquisition of literacy in patriotic terms:

> I returned to Arkansas and followed your suggestion. I found a job and edu-
> cated myself when I was not working. I have studied American history, which
> was your suggestion. Learning to read and write is knowing America, my
> country. Knowing America is actually knowing myself. Knowing myself is
> also knowing how to serve my country. Now I'm serving her. (248)

Custer's story implies that American identity is not founded solely on biological inheritance, but emerges through proper training. More than figuring
a Filipino as a spokesperson of U.S. ideology, this scene transforms a colonial
trope—education—that links Filipinos and American culture into a component of postwar U.S. identity. Perhaps it is because Bulosan was constructing

an implied narrative of origin for Carlos that the U.S. narrative of biological origin is reimagined in this episode. By referring to Custer's recognized status as a U.S. citizen, Bulosan contrasts it with the liminal status of Filipinos. This episode highlights Carlos's contributions to Custer's progress in a way that points back to the limited mobility and employment opportunities that Filipinos confront as colonized subjects and U.S. nationals.

We need to understand Bulosan's authorial position as the outcome of a complex negotiation. To explain his critique of Luce's "American Century," my readings attend to the ways in which it had to engage an emergent discourse of the professional expert as the privileged U.S. citizen–subject. As Filipinos find jobs in the newly inclusive U.S. defense industries and armed forces during World War II, Carlos identifies the changing status of Filipinos as part of a global shift: "Our world was this one, but a new one was being born. We belonged to the old world of confusion; but in this other world— new, bright, promising—we would be unable to meet its demands" (324). By adapting Luce's postwar rhetoric, Carlos recovers the prewar forms of belonging that were available to Filipinos as colonized nationals who could lay claim to a "special" relationship with the United States. His vision of the uncertain postwar status of Filipinos might be seen, then, as both a counterpart of and counterpoint to Luce's American century.

Bulosan suggests the need to frame the watershed event of World War II as a story that is shaped by conceptions of Filipinos as racial problems and solutions rather than progress narratives that center on colonialism and independence or immigration and assimilation. To explain the significance of this reframing, let me turn to the representation of this historical juncture in the strangely optimistic ending of *America Is in the Heart*. When Carlos pays his brother's shoeshine debt, the Negro bootblack underscores the significance of this act by committing Carlos's brother to memory: "Even if I don't see him again, I'll remember him whenever I see the face of an American dime" (324). As the legal and political status of Filipinos shifts from colonized national to potential citizen, the bootblack implicitly voices its broader impact. Bulosan uses this scene to link Filipino and African Americans as exploited labor that underwrites U.S. economic power, but also to suggest that the reclassification of Filipinos as Asian immigrants is also a reconfiguration of relations among Filipinos, African Americans, and American capital.

Even as Carlos registers the democratic reforms that open new employment sectors for Filipinos and enable their incorporation into dominant nationalist narratives during World War II, he specifically frames them as a disruption to the bonds between Filipino writers and workers. The closing snapshot of Carlos gazing out of a bus window at Filipino pea pickers in the fields showcases the relationship between the Filipino writer and workers, but also indicates its uncertain future. So imagined, the Filipino writer prefigures the cultural broker, a key fixture in model minority discourse that defines and manages the terms by which knowledge is produced in ways that benefit him and advance a particular social vision.[32] Although conceptions of Asian Americans as a model minority are conventionally understood as the result of 1965 immigration policy and a reaction to the intensification of black civil rights and protest movements, Bulosan provides us with a glimpse of the emergence of a model minority discourse as it takes shape in the shadow of black pathologization, the transformation of the U.S.–Philippines colonial relationship, and U. S. immigration narratives during World War II.

I have used Bulosan to suggest that the elevation of a liberal discourse on race helped to legitimate the critical turn to a professional citizen–subject in U.S. cultural politics exemplified by Luce's emergent technocracy. Through Carlos's transformation into a writer, Bulosan accomplishes a reorientation of the narrative of progress outlined by Luce. What enables Bulosan to revise the ontological status of Filipinos under benevolent assimilation is his specific engagement with sociological studies of the Filipino race problem as the official discourse on race. As Bulosan appropriates sociological ways of seeing in order to question the gaze of sociological studies of race, he simultaneously renounces its explanatory authority in favor of a redefined progress narrative and Filipino writer. Whereas Bulosan proposes a professional Filipino knowledge producer as an expert on Americanization, Jade Snow Wong, a Chinese American writer, presents the figure of a Chinese American female artist–entrepreneur as emerging in relation to Luce's powerful vision of a globally oriented technocracy in Asia and racial pathologies of the Chinese "coolie" and "prostitute." As we will see in chapter 4, Wong reframes constructions of Asian American women as global symbols of racial progress in a way that questions the masculine bias of an emergent U.S. nationalist discourse of Asian American citizenship.

4.

Not Black, Not Coolies

Pathologization, Asian American Citizenship, and
Jade Snow Wong's Fifth Chinese Daughter

In 1945, Jade Snow Wong installed her potter's wheel in a busy Grant Avenue storefront window and began throwing down clay. Described by the San
Francisco media as an Oriental spectacle, a "wonder in the eyes of the Western world," she created a sensation, drawing crowds of spectators, night and
day. In her numerous public statements and writings, Wong returns again and
again to the shop window, remembering her live display as a critical turning
point that transformed her from a Chinatown eccentric into an artist–entrepreneur, renowned author, and eventually a cultural ambassador for the U.S.
State Department.

But despite her mainstream success, what mattered most to Wong were
the skeptical and scandalized reactions of Chinese businessmen. In her autobiography *Fifth Chinese Daughter* (1950), she foregrounds their perceptions
of her professional debut: "Chinatown was agog. A woman in the window,
her legs astride a potter's wheel, her hair in braids, her hands perpetually
messy with sticky California clay, her finished products such things as coolies
used in China, the daughter of a conservative family, running a business
alone—such a combination was sure to fail!"[1] By emphasizing their interpretation of her live display as a sexualized spectacle, a "woman in the window,"
she positions the figure of the artist–entrepreneur at odds with a Chinatown
community that stressed middle-class aspirations and respectable femininity.[2]
According to Wong, Chinatown merchants saw her as an abnormal woman

because of her efforts to establish a business alone, but specifically targeted her strategy of charging higher prices for her "primitive" pottery than the going rates for what they saw as the obligatory Chinese porcelain that featured painted golden dragons and other exotic, "Oriental" designs. Indeed, Wong uses this scene to demonstrate her attempt to redefine the criteria for what was to be seen as Chinese and to turn a profit, while also positioning her vision at odds with the Chinatown business community.

Fifth Chinese Daughter is an account of Wong's life from the age of four to twenty-four in San Francisco's Chinatown and Bay Area and centers particularly on her education from elementary school through the years directly following her graduation from Mills College. Though it continues to be read and taught as a story about generational conflict in an immigrant family and the struggle to maintain Chinese traditions and assimilate into mainstream U.S. society, Wong's autobiography is predominantly seen as a model minority narrative and Wong herself as an inept writer and state tool.

Such positions, I believe, have minimized the significance that Wong attributes to her live display and contributed to misreadings of it as just another example of her desire to win the approval of the white world by fashioning herself as the quintessential "American" entrepreneur in the image of a white self-made man. These views are also encouraged by the illustration that accompanies Wong's text, which depicts the divergent reactions to her live display through the figures of a man hoisting himself onto a telephone pole to obtain a better view and a bespectacled, well-dressed Chinese man turning his back on Wong to emphasize her rejection by the Chinatown community and growing popularity in the white world.

But as I argue, Wong is more interested in investigating the Otherness of the figure of the Chinese woman. Her rich, if compressed, description of her live display brings into focus the logic by which mainstream U.S. society saw the integration of Chinese women into the U.S. nation as a democratic legal reform that would stabilize Chinese American middle-class formation and facilitate, more generally, U.S. racial progress and global ascendancy.[3] What happens, I ask, when we consider the sexualized image in the window that Wong actually describes rather than the illustration of Wong as a petite, modestly dressed Chinese woman shaping a pot in front of an enormous crowd? In calling attention to the presence of the Chinatown business community, Wong's self-description and vivid image give voice to their strong disapproval of the public spectacle of a Chinese woman and negative perception of "coolies" in China. Defined by its intertwined interests in promoting respectable femininity and distancing itself from China's proletariat, the Chinatown business community might be seen as a parallel formation to the figure of the Chinese woman, both emerging in relation to a cold war discourse of Asian American citizenship. For Wong, the figure of the Chinese woman takes shape from the intersection of three geopolitical currents: the rise of the Asian American citizen, U.S. postwar political interests in Asia, and the postwar racialization of Asian Americans as "not black" (in opposition to pathological conceptions of African Americans) and as modernizing subjects (in contrast to the counterconstruction of "coolies" in China).

This chapter investigates how the figure of the artist–entrepreneur became a compelling way for Wong to revise dominant narratives of postwar Chinese American progress. Wong specifically traces the emergence of a figure defined by the capacity to conduct research and organize information that could counter primitivist stereotypes of Chinese and limiting class and gender norms for Chinese women. Chinese women were significant not only to the U.S. ability to demonstrate that it was taking steps to reform racism by lifting exclusion laws, but also to the construction of Chinese Americans as symbols and agents of the renewal of the U.S. national polity. Indeed, the World War II transformation of the Chinese from foreign aliens to potential citizens was envisioned as a sexual and gendering process, characterized by the U.S. extensions of the naturalization process to Chinese Americans and the War Brides Act to Asian American veterans. The increased presence of Chinese women in the United States could thus be seen as a barometer of the degree to which wartime reforms were improving race relations overall.[4]

To emphasize the structural impact of the regulation of Chinese female immigration, Wong had to disrupt dominant understandings of Chinese women as complements to the lifting of Chinese exclusion laws or as another step forward in the teleological narrative of Chinese American uplift. I argue that Wong's focus on the figure of the artist–entrepreneur provided her with a way to highlight the significance of Chinese women to the geopolitical question of whether Chinese Americans were to be seen as conduits toward U.S. postwar progress and economic expansion or throwbacks to the prewar era of racial exclusion and U.S. provincialism.[5] Situating her figure of the artist–entrepreneur in relation to narratives of U.S. global expansion in Asia complicates our understanding of World War II reforms by placing it in the same discursive universe as liberal narratives of U.S. immigration and Asian American citizenship that centered primarily on the experiences of Asian American male veterans. At the same time, this interpretive move offers us a more complex

view of Asian American writers as cultural producers who selectively negotiated historic and representational conventions in an emergent liberal discourse
of which they were a part.

The Immigrant We All Are Looking For

In adapting the historic figures of the Chinese prostitute and the coolie for
the postwar and early cold war context of Asian American citizenship, Wong
highlights the persistent ambiguities over Asian racial identity that followed
the Chinese, even after they were no longer legally aliens. Doing so meant
that she could show how Chinese American subject formations develop
through arguments on irregular labor and the figure of the Chinese woman.
Drawing on sexually explicit imagery, she depicts herself as a "woman in the
window" with her legs straddling the pottery wheel, thus evoking nineteenth-
century stereotypes of publicly visible Chinese women as "Chinese prostitutes" performing illicit labor. In mimicking elite Chinese perceptions of her
pottery as "such things as coolies used in China," she also indicates how and
why an expanding Chinese American middle class constructed coolies as
premodern, foreign Chinese to indigenize themselves as Californians and displace historic figurations of the Chinese coolie as a California race problem.
Evoking nineteenth-century pathologies of Chinese as unsettling reminders
of arguments that assisted in the definition of Chinese as an "unassimilable"
racial group in U.S. society, Wong showcases her capacity to analyze and
transform them into what she sees as more acceptable signifiers of postwar
Chinese American progress.

Condemning coolies worked multiple ideological fronts in the nineteenth
century as racial projects that were antislavery, supportive of U.S. imperial
expansion into Asia and the Americas, and pro (white European) immigrant.[6] In the post-exclusion era for Asian Americans, the racial image of
coolies, as the embodiment of coerced labor and reminder of the U.S. history
of slavery, threatened critically important constructions of the United States
as a democratic space of "free" immigrant individuals. By recovering pathologized figures of the coolie and the Chinese prostitute that were centrally
constitutive of nineteenth-century stereotypes of Chinese as immoral and
enslaved, Wong alludes to the way in which racial pathologies that compared
Asian Americans and black Americans haunted the lives of Chinese Americans and complicated the developmental narrative of national progress. Her
text offers us a glimpse of the processes by which Orientalist conceptions

of culture identified Asian Americans and African Americans as racially marked groups while also defining divergent cultural destinies for them.[7]

By adapting the dichotomy of coolies and immigrants to the discourses of postwar Asian American citizenship and U.S. nationalism, Wong defines her figure of the artist–entrepreneur as Chinese American. In the context of early cold war anticommunism, Wong calls attention to the way in which Chinese Americans negotiated their contested status as potential citizens by framing the coolie problem as a mainland Chinese affront to Chinese American standards of labor and respectable domesticity. By locating coolies in China, Wong also distinguishes her artisan pottery from mass-produced coolie products.[8]

To situate the postwar racialization of Asian Americans as emerging from the shift from biological notions of race to a cultural concept of ethnicity, Wong demonstrates how the incorporation of Asians into the United States encouraged identification with white European immigrant groups that had become synonymous with conceptions of "ordinary Americans" and postwar U.S. national identity. By indicating how Chinese self-identification as U.S. "immigrants" also worked as claims to a privileged status attributed to white European immigrants, Wong suggests that it likewise distanced Chinese from other racialized communities of color.

In taking inventory of her various viewing publics, Wong also notes that the police are among her first spectators, remarking that they came "because they thought there might be a riot" (244). The manner in which police initially perceive a mass gathering in Chinatown as potentially violent and criminal is revealing. By calling attention to the police presence rather than cropping them from the frame, Wong locates the racialization of Asian Americans as war-minded Orientals in the same discursive universe as the racial violence erupting in U.S. cities from Los Angeles to New York, including the 1943 zoot suit riots in military towns along the Pacific Coast. This scene registers the contradictory messages regarding perceptions of Asian Americans that viewed Chinese and Mexican Indians as both coming from a violent "Oriental" civilization that was disrespectful of human life, but that also implied that only "Orientals" possessed the cultural potential to be "domesticated," as they were seen to be naturally more law-abiding than Mexicans and African Americans.[9]

By raising the specter of race riots, Wong implicitly contrasts the curiosity that her live display aroused in Chinese merchants and non-Chinese spectators to the moral panic over juvenile delinquency that the race riots symbolized and were believed to intensify. As Stuart Cosgrove observes, wartime statistics illuminated new patterns of adolescent behavior at the same time that the term "delinquency" emerged from the lexicon of sociology and made its way into common parlance.[10] By situating the emergence of the artist–entrepreneur in the same discursive universe as the rise of the Asian American citizen and the development of theories of delinquent citizens, Wong reveals the comparative race context that underwrites the production of "loyal" Asian Americans.

In my reading of Wong's live display, I have suggested that she asserted herself politically in a less obvious fashion by transforming a Chinatown shop window into a profitable public stage. In contrast to zoot suiters that claimed the public spaces of the streets and destabilized the boundaries mandated by segregation and class in highly visible ways, Wong redefined the historic association of public visibility for Chinese women in Chinatown with prostitution and Oriental depravity, but used it to articulate an alternative vision of postwar progress.[11] Through the artist–entrepreneur, she articulates a gendered form of alien citizenship. At the moment that the legal and political status of Chinese Americans is shifting from depraved foreign aliens to potential citizens, Wong offers us a glimpse of the processes of Asian American racialization that involve the figuration of Chinese as Asian "immigrants," the redefinition of middle-class gender norms, and the counterconstruction of African Americans and Mexican Americans as delinquent citizens.

Postwar Alien Citizenship

By taking up the very figures that symbolized uncivilized and immoral Chinese, Wong brings into relief the contested terms and implications of Chinese incorporation into the U.S. nation.[12] She frustrates the assumption that the recasting of Chinese as deserving citizens by wartime reforms is a fait accompli. Such assumptions impede the kind of representational complexity and authority that Wong will later demand. Indeed, the shift to Asian American citizenship did not consign such problems or racial pathologies as the Chinese prostitute and coolie to the past, but rather haunted the possibilities, contexts, and pressures for Chinese American claims to citizenship and belonging. Suggesting a congruence between the artist–entrepreneur and earlier figures of the coolie and the Chinese prostitute enables Wong to reflect upon the gendered implications of changing conceptions of Chinese from diseased coolies to deserving citizens during the early cold war as the United States is looking to expand its political and economic influence in decolonizing nations.[13]

Despite dominant conceptions of World War II as a watershed period for communities of color, the demographic and economic changes brought about by the war heightened existing racial conflicts and increased class tensions within urban communities.[14] In particular, World War II and the cold war produced new iterations of alien citizenship and generated tensions within the Chinese American and Japanese American communities as well as conflicts between Asian Americans and the U.S. government. As Mae Ngai has argued, alien citizenship refers to a "condition of racial otherness, a badge of foreignness that could not be shed," and was a key concept in the formation of U.S. race policies that included the forced repatriation of almost a half million Mexicans during the Great Depression and the Japanese American internment. For example, Asian Americans and Mexican Americans born in the United States possessed formal U.S. citizenship, but were alien citizens in the sense that they continued to be seen by the mainstream U.S. nation as permanently foreign and unassimilable.[15] If the legal and cultural construction of Asians as permanent foreigners had been shaped by more than half a century of exclusion laws, then World War II and the cold war infused that foreignness with new political meanings and created the framework for defining U.S. citizenship for the generation that was born in the United States as well as the social location of Asian Americans.[16] The meanings of citizenship continued to change as U.S. political and military allegiances in East Asia were realigned after World War II and through the cold war as China became the Communist enemy after the Chinese Revolution and a reconstructed Japan became America's postwar ally.

To understand the reach of "alien citizen" beyond legal and political consideration, Robert Lee looks to the ways in which cultural notions of difference structure understandings of what it means to be alien: "Alienness is both a formal political or legal status and an informal, but by no means less powerful, cultural status. The two states are hardly synonymous or congruent. Alien legal status and the procedures by which it can be shed often depend on the cultural definitions of difference."[17] To understand how the transformation of foreign and degenerate Chinese into normative subjects and potential citizens generated new forms of alien citizenship, Wong rethinks this shift in terms of the gendered forms of Asian racialization rather than the reform of racism. The emphasis on racial reform, as she implies, produces an exclusionary and foundational narrative of Asian American citizenship oriented toward Asian American men. Rather than envisioning the figure of the artist–entrepreneur as a symbol of her personal success, Wong sees it as part of a racialized critique of the dominant narrative of U.S. racial reform and national progress that constructs Chinese women as the liber-ated subjects of U.S. democracy and symbols of racial progress. To engage the overlap between U.S. economic expansion and the rising currency of Asian Americans, Wong articulates a narrative of Asian American citizenship and U.S. postwar progress that features a Chinese American female artist–entrepreneur as the principal agent.

Interpreting Wong's text as pursuing only an Anglo-European immigrant narrative misses how it specifically develops a racialized gendered narrative of Asian American citizenship. Indeed, Wong figures her work as the object of speculation and inquiry from other Chinese, engaging ethnicity in a way that puts askew the prevailing narratives of Asian American citizenship and U.S. racial progress that took their legitimacy and power from a history of immigration reform that centers primarily on Asian American men, includ-ing the repeal of Chinese exclusion laws under the 1943 Magnuson Act, the opening of employment in defense industries and the armed forces, the extension of the 1945 War Brides Act to Asian American veterans in 1947, broader access to bank loans, and increased opportunities to purchase homes in integrated areas and, through the support of the 1944 GI Bill, obtain a college education.[18] Wong's figure of the artist–entrepreneur points back to middle-class Chinese anxiety over the seemingly unfixed place of Chinese American women in a changing landscape of Asian American citizenship and postwar U.S. global expansion. Yet she also positions the artist–entrepre-neur as an alternative to the limited opportunities and restricted mobility for Asian American women in a racially stratified labor market and also to the prevailing discourse of Chinese American progress in which Chinese women are incorporated into the U.S. nation as dependent citizens and war brides and Chinese men as veterans and homeowners.

Emerging at a time when an ethnicity concept of race and the U.S. war-time alliance of China and the Philippines had generated a demand for eth-nic narratives by Asian American writers, *Fifth Chinese Daughter* is often seen as belonging to a genre of Chinatown stories that includes Pardee Lowe's *Father and Glorious Descendant* (1943) and C. Y. Lee's *Flower Drum Song* (1957).[19] In claiming that these Asian American writings of the 1940s and 1950s are not, in fact, American stories, recent studies have offered analyses of how such texts develop the intersections between U.S. domestic racial politics and cold war foreign policy by staging narratives about assimilation in a U.S. global context of the cold war. To explain how conceptions of Asian American writings as texts that are centrally about the U.S. incorpo-ration of Asian immigrant groups produce narrow readings, Christina Klein shows how such positions obstruct understandings of their dual, global role as "domestic counterparts" to postwar writings on international tourism in Asia. Chinatown stories such as Wong's text, she contends, not only emphasize the similarity between the experiences of Chinese Americans and white European immigrants, but also work to close the gap between Americans and "a people whose integration has become a geopolitical imperative" (228).[20] For Klein, what gave Chinese American writers such as Wong value as "Americans" during the 1940s and 1950s was the notion of their dual identity, or "partial foreignness," which made them ideal candidates for performing their assimilation into U.S. society in a way that could simultaneously legitimate U.S. claims to internationalism as the embodiment of what Carey McWilliams termed a "nation of nations."[21] By framing Chinese American writers as both assimilated Chinese Americans and transnational subjects, Klein raises critically important questions about the relationship between U.S. racial discourse and foreign policy, but also constructs writers such as Wong as appropriated objects within hegemonic U.S. nationalist discourses. How might situating Wong's live display in a global frame, as emerging from the intersection of U.S. racial politics, postwar progress, and cold war policy, open questions about Chinese Americans as social actors?[22]

Remarking on representations of the figure of the Chinatown bachelor in Chinatown stories by Wong and other contemporaneous writers, Elaine Kim observes that they appear to be more of a formal exercise than of genuine interest, "as if their creators were aware of their presence but had little interest in their real lives. Certainly most second-generation Chinese Americans met such persons every day. But Lowe, Wong, and Lee express little interest in them beyond their value as interesting character sketches to be appended to descriptions of customs, festivals, and artifacts that make up the Chinese American community they present for the reader's edification."[23] By interpreting the inclusion of the Chinese bachelor as a superficial feature intended to enhance the text's mainstream and ethnographic appeal, Kim misses how Wong's representation indicates the need for new analytic approaches. In her profile of Uncle Kwok, her father's factory employee, Wong affirms the significance of the bachelor figure to studies of the Oriental problem, but also depicts him as emerging from processes that cannot be easily or fully explained. While social scientists, politicians, and the popular media employed racial stereotypes of disease and sexual degeneracy to depict Chinese bachelors as a social threat, Wong depicts Uncle Kwok as part of a workforce that emerges from historical conditions and individual agency. Though Jade Snow retains her role as a privileged observer by continuing to survey this figure from a distance, she indicates the limits of such sociological methods by noting that she "never found an answer that satisfied her."[24]

In proposing the artist–entrepreneur (rather than the Chinese bachelor or veteran) as the paradigmatic postwar figure, *Fifth Chinese Daughter* is able to consider how the extension of the legal category and discourse of the U.S. immigrant to Chinese Americans shaped the terms of Chinese American women's claims of belonging and citizenship. If legal reforms such as the GI Bill led to greater accessibility to a university education and homeowner loans shaped the cultural and political discourse for Asian American men's claims to U.S. citizenship and forms of belonging, then what discourses were available to Chinese American women such as Wong?

A "Globally Oriented" Technocracy

Wong's figure of the artist–entrepreneur offers a contemporary glimpse of the moment in which cultural producers in the United States envisioned postwar progress as the dissemination of globally oriented, U.S.-educated professionals and knowledge practices in Asia. To propose the Chinese American female artist–entrepreneur as the ideal postwar citizen–subject, Wong first had to engage contemporaneous arguments that portrayed Asia as a postwar frontier that was critical to U.S. aspirations of global leadership. When Henry Luce envisioned Asia as the stage for "the American Century" as a U.S.-dominated postwar era during the early part of 1941, he specifically outlined a process by which the United States could adopt the broader economic perspective necessary to expand its reach into Asian markets and manifest its destiny as a postwar global leader rather than resign itself to a state of "pitiful impotence."[25] Conceptualizing Asia as an exploitable resource was, as Luce saw it, the proper perspective for understanding the U.S. role in the postwar global order. Closely tied to this model for U.S. economic expansion, he explains, is a U.S.-trained technocracy, a set of globally oriented experts that could convey a "picture of an America" and produce the conditions that would enable the United States to accept its destined role of global leadership.[26]

Almost a decade later, the bestselling travel writer James Michener reworked Luce's figuration of globally oriented experts as the centerpiece of his vision of a postwar technocracy by identifying Asian racial formations in Hawaii as a valuable resource for building U.S. relationships with Asia. In making Hawaii central to U.S. attempts to imagine its postwar relationship with Asia, Michener and other proponents of Hawaiian statehood saw the large populations of Asians in Hawaii as a strategic resource that could pro-vide the United States with a "unique medium of communication and under-standing with Asiatic peoples."[27] To engage conceptions of Asia as the U.S. postwar frontier, Wong combined Luce's emphasis on U.S.-trained profes-sionals with contemporaneous figurations that linked Asian racial formations and U.S. economic expansion in Asia in order to insert a narrative about a Chinese American female artist–entrepreneur into the postwar global order. In envisioning the Chinese female artist–entrepreneur as paradigmatic post-war technocrat, Wong reconfigured Luce's emphasis on U.S.-trained, globally oriented professionals to open up a critique of gender and ethnicity. Doing so meant that Wong positioned the artist–entrepreneur within a discourse of U.S. nationalism that simultaneously excluded contemporaneous racialized migrants that included Mexican *braceros* and Chinese Marxists, who were increasingly subject to official scrutiny and expulsion in the anti-Communist cold war climate of the United States.[28] In taking the form of a coming-of-age narrative, Wong's text intersects wartime discourses on rebellious youth, including the identification of new patterns in adolescent behavior by sociologists and the mainstream media in their attempts to link a culture of delinquency to African American and Mexican poverty. In positioning her figure of the artist–entrepreneur within a global discourse that focused on U.S. professionals in Asia, she references and distances this figure from wartime discourses of delinquency and Asian American citizenship.

Fifth Chinese Daughter specifically engages arguments on the convergence between U.S. postwar economic expansion in Asia and the rising currency of U.S.-educated Asian American women in the context of a liberal triumph of ethnicity. Rather than treating the postwar focus on university-educated Asian American women as a coincidence, the book instead advanced notions of the "modern success" of Asian American women and helped to mask U.S. political and economic domination in Asia as democratic and cultur-ally beneficial for everyone involved. As Shirley J. Lim notes, education was critical to the display of cold war citizenship; Asian American newspapers often featured accomplished young women, particularly university students, as emblems of modernity and the legitimacy of decolonization.[29]

U.S. popular media portrayed Wong as a successful woman of color who could testify to the attention and recognition she had received from Ameri-can institutions and the state. She was constructed as a successful Asian who would ensure that ancient Oriental traditions would continue to flour-ish in modern American society. Even though Wong's text foregrounds her

innovativeness and strategic self-fashioning as well as her difficulties in sav-
ing money for school and starting a business, U.S. magazines depicted her
as an exotic Oriental producer of "exquisite ceramics." In an article on the
growing metropolis of San Francisco, *National Geographic* (August 1956)
included a photograph of Wong at her pottery wheel under the heading "An
Ancient Art of China Finds Modern Expression," with accompanying text
that portrayed her as a success story in an America that valued Chinese
artistic traditions—or at least the ones that were not Communist.[30] Such
representations stressed the foreignness of Chinese Americans such as Wong
to emphasize the notion that "traditional" Chinese art flourished under U.S.
democracy and was key to U.S. efforts to cast itself as having a particular
capacity for appreciating and preserving China's rich cultural history. Even
more specifically, depicting accomplished Chinese American women as car-
riers of ethnic artistic traditions and as the liberated objects of U.S. immigration reform provided a way for the United States to emphasize its progress in
race relations and also portray itself as a democratic, cultural pluralist nation
in the face of Communist tyranny.[31] In the early years of the cold war, the
U.S. nation asserted itself as a global leader by contrasting "American standards of labor" to those in totalitarian societies.

Strangeness in Chinatown

Wong's text registers an important shift in conceptions of Chinatown in the
mid-twentieth century as it increasingly came to be seen as a tourist destination rather than a vice district. The Chinatown that appears in *Fifth Chinese
Daughter* is a changing community shaped by a series of international events,
including the Sino-Japanese War that brings Jade Snow's elder siblings back
to San Francisco, as well as World War II restrictions on commercial ship-
ping that blocked further imports of the goods and foods that Chinatown
had historically depended upon for commerce and daily living. For Wong,
the impact of World War II manifested itself not only in legal reforms that
opened the naturalization process to Asian immigrants, but also in the redefinition of Chinatown as a tourist bazaar rather than as a strictly Chinese commercial zone: "The mellow look in Chinese stores gave way to a bazaar aspect
as display gaps were filled with Mexican pottery and glass, glittering costume
jewelry, flimsy baskets, and humorous souvenirs. But the eager tourists with
the flush pockets of 1944 created enough of a demand to make Chinatown
an economically prosperous community" (211).

Wong's story in *Fifth Chinese Daughter* exemplifies the crossroads between the sociological production of racial and cultural difference and the cold war commodification of racial and cultural difference. By figuring herself as the object of curiosity and speculation in her live display, Wong is also able to position herself as an informed analyst of each episode. In depicting the attempts of Chinese shop owners to decipher the secret to her business success, Wong points out how they perceive the male shopkeeper as the proper authority and businessman:

> Some Chinese approached the proprietor for information. Was it because her clay came from China? Was it because she had invented a new chemical process to make pottery? The proprietor would smile politely. "Ask her," he would say. But no one ever asked her. Chinese and Americans alike acted as if they thought she were deaf or dumb or couldn't understand their language. (244–45)

This scene is representative of a central problem for Wong: the failure of public recognition and financial profit to transform her into an expert knower. By juxtaposing the dehumanizing treatment that she receives from Chinese business owners against the stereotypes of Orientals as primitive Others that white spectators use to interpret her work, Wong points to the limits of the public appeal of her pottery. Recounting the ways in which she is perceived as an object enables her to consider how knowledge and professional expertise are specifically racialized and gendered.

Taking on the persona of an analyst also prepares Jade Snow to evaluate her critics from what she sees as a superior and more informed perspective. In depicting herself as a spectacularized object, she transforms what may have been hurtful personal knowledge into a demonstration of the broader, systemic understanding that she possesses and that her critics presumably lack. For Wong, the way in which viewers speculate about her work as if she were not present leads to the development of universalized knowledge, an understanding of "a very curious thing about human beings" rather than self-knowledge about an isolated incident (245). Though the success of her live display does not change how she is viewed as a skilled artist or authority on her work, it provides her with a site for comparing the reactions of her viewing publics and asserting her knowledge as a product of her artistic training, business strategy, and U.S. location rather than her biological makeup or ethnic upbringing. Describing how viewers speculate about her pottery also allows her to reference the commercial demand for "Oriental" objects such as porcelain and rice bowls that contribute to such perceptions: "People would talk about me as if my presence were not there, and they never thought to ask me for the explanation—that there were no porcelain clays in California and I made one-of-a-kind pieces, not sets of rice bowls."[32] By considering how she too is seen as an exotic, inanimate object, Wong asserts her explanation to their queries; she positions her "formula" and "hidden secrets" as the results of her professional training in pottery and in the lessons in operating a business that she picked up from her association with a pottery guild (238). Displacing the figure of the Chinese coolie, or mass producer that was symbolically congruent with the stereotype of the communist, allows Wong to claim the status of a Chinese American artist–entrepreneur. Such links between Wong's figure of the artist–entrepreneur as emerging from a larger context that references wartime immigration reforms and the growing anti-Communist climate are made clear in her account of the shifts in orientation from a future in strengthening China to starting her own business in the United States. For Wong, the figure of the artist–entrepreneur emerges from a reconfigured liberal narrative of Chinese American progress, which turned on the notion that the Chinese had proven themselves as loyal U.S. subjects during wartime, reformed their communities, and could now be seen as "deserving citizens," entitled to federal resources and recognition such as public housing and citizenship.

Articulating "Cultured Orientals": The Politics of Racial Redemption

To more fully explain the intersections between the processes of objectification, comparative racialization, and professionalization, I will briefly discuss the ascendance of sociology to the status of official discourse on race. By the mid-1940s, the field of sociology was the dominant producer of knowledge on race and racism and had assumed an increasingly important role in imagining the trajectory of the nation's future. In the 1920s, sociologists collected stories about the lives of racial minorities in the United States as part of their research on race relations and ordered their personal memories and experiences into a set of standard narratives based on categories. Assisted by sociologists' own retellings of them within academia, these sociological narratives became synonymous with the expression of ethnicity and over time shaped U.S. understandings of race and ethnicity.[33] Sociology produced a particular discourse around race in the early twentieth century that provided people of color with a sanctioned language for identifying and analyzing the conditions of their objectification but after World War II outlined a specific role for Asian Americans. By calling into question the assumption that Asian

American citizenship had resolved the Oriental race problem, Wong examines the processes through which postwar Asian American racialization took shape in relation to counterconstructions of African Americans. Sociology was the dominant discourse that identified Asians and African Americans as racially marked while also defining them as groups with divergent cultural destinies. Indeed, the professionalizing possibilities that sociological studies of race held out to Orientals were intertwined with processes of comparative racialization and a concept of culture that was increasingly invoked as a corrective to biologically based notions of race. In emphasizing the concept of culture, the figure of the "racial uniform" also effaces the historical origins of the production of difference by rendering them as fixed categories. The combined discourses surrounding U.S. postwar expansion in Asia and the notion of a U.S.-trained global technocracy also gave sharper definition to the professionalizing possibilities that sociological studies of race opened to Asian Americans. Considering postwar Asian American racialization, black pathologization, and the ascendance of a global U.S.-trained technocracy as part of the same postwar discursive universe allows a clearer understanding of the dual processes of the "liberal hegemony" of sociological studies and the production of the Asian American citizen.

Robert E. Park's 1914 metaphor of the "racial uniform" for the status of the Oriental exemplifies the crossroads between comparative racialization and a culture concept of race.[34] Used in his theory of racial assimilation, Park's under-studied image is most obviously meant to refer to the biological racial discourse that limits the life chances of racialized groups. Both African Americans and Asian Americans wear the "racial uniform," he explains, suggesting that it comprises the primary obstacle to an assimilation process modeled on white ethnic groups. At the same time, however, Park argues that only Asian Americans, if given the opportunity by whites, possess the capacity to culturally assimilate. Perhaps the familiarity of Park's figure is its resemblance to contemporary notions of a model minority. The "racial uniform" alludes to a process by which sociological theories of race assign an exemplary status to Asian Americans that is underwritten by denigrating pathologies of African Americans and conceptions of Asian Americans as foreign outsiders.

As a corollary to Park's figure of the racial uniform, Gunnar Myrdal argued that African Americans were—in comparison to Chinese and Japanese—"more helplessly imprisoned as a subordinate caste in America, a caste of people deemed to be lacking a cultural past and assumed to be incapable of a cultural future." Elaborating on Park's comparative race paradigm, Myrdal's influential study *An American Dilemma: The Negro Problem and Modern American Democracy* (1944) also employed many of Park's former students and was one of the markers of the way in which ethnicity, as a cultural concept of race, had come to define postwar discourse on race. To redeem Asian Americans as "cultured Orientals," Myrdal simultaneously defined African Americans as exceptionally pathological, positioning them on the other side of the spectrum of racial pathologies.

The coupling of the sociology of race and Wong's autobiography presents interesting moments in the history of the relationship between fiction writing and the production of racial knowledge. While this comparative and racist ideology is one that Wong, in a sense, draws from Park and Myrdal, it is also one that she uses to flesh out a new form of authority for Asian Americans. Her text shows how the processes by which Chinese Americans are interpellated by sociological representations of race are the same ones that positioned Asian Americans at the top of a hierarchy of racial pathologies. Such links between racial pathologies and the figuration of Asian Americans as analysts of race are made clear in a scene in which a young Jade Snow asks her mother where babies come from. Framed as a tactful reply to what might be seen as a universal "growing up" question, Mama puts forth a theory of comparative racialization: "There are three kinds of babies. When they are nearly done, they are white foreign babies. When they bake a little longer, they become golden Chinese babies. Sometimes they are left in too long, and they become black babies!"(24) Defining racial identity as a work in progress, Chinese emerge as the ideal, white as "not quite complete," and blacks as irreparably damaged. Wong uses this moment to present a Chinese immigrant as a knowledge producer of race, but even more important to give greater emphasis to the role of a Chinese American figure in evaluating the racial views held by their parents. As Wong tells it, Jade Snow "turned over this information in her mind, and concluded that it was quite reasonable" (24). By separating knowledge production from the tasks of evaluation and dissemination, Wong identifies a specific and privileged function for second-generation Chinese Americans who are depicted as giving order and legitimacy to the knowledge produced by the older generation of Chinese immigrants.

Academic Sociology

By taking into account processes of knowledge production about Chinese and Chinese American subject formation, sociology opened up possibilities for self-understanding to Wong and others in ways that coincided with professional advancement and official recognition at U.S. universities, but that also demonstrated the limits of such mobility. Though Wong was not among the Americanized Oriental university students who participated in race relations surveys and undertook graduate study in sociology, she calls attention to her discovery of sociology as a critical introduction to modes of inquiry, frameworks of evaluation, and standard narratives of academic sociology of race. In depicting herself as an interpreter of race, Wong situates herself as part of a context that requires her to negotiate sociological theories and her parents' vision of the world.

Her text offers a detailed account of how U.S. universities were the principal sites that gave value to her self-understanding as Chinese American. Tempting as it may be to read Wong's observations that she received higher grades when she wrote about Chinatown or Chinese culture as a generic desire for recognition from the white world or evidence of her co-optation into a model minority role, we also need to consider how the pleasure that Wong takes from her academic work stems from writing "about Chinatown and the people that she had known all her life" (132). Through her college courses in sociology, Wong comes to understand that the things and people that she might otherwise perceive as uninteresting or peculiar only to her life were considered exotic and of scientific value to her professors and other authority figures at the university. Furthermore, as Henry Yu observes, in framing particular kinds of knowledge about Orientals as exotic information, sociologists also defined for Asian Americans such as Wong what it meant to be an intellectual in the United States.[35] Wong signifies on sociology's aesthetic principles and authority when she describes how she challenged her parents' rules by "suppressing all anger, and in a manner that would have done credit to her sociology instructor addressing his freshman class" (128). After becoming a sociology major, Jade Snow defines "good writing" as an artistic improvement on the factual reporting she had done in her diaries (132).

Wong's account of her experiences as a U.S. university student symbolized the social contradictions operating in and reconstituted by the post–World War II period. As she tells it, her incorporation into the university is intertwined with her entry into domestic service: "Because I was female, my parents would not support my college education. So, I cooked, cleaned houses, and took care of children in after-school classes for income to cover two years of junior college." In emphasizing the racialized and gendered terms that define Jade Snow's path to college, Wong describes the transformative effect of her introduction to sociology in junior college:

But if Latin was the easiest course and chemistry the most difficult, sociology was the most stimulating. Jade Snow had chosen it without thought, simply to meet a requirement, but that casual decision completely revolutionized her thinking, shattering her Wong-constructed conception of the order of things. (124)

Sociology enables Jade Snow to envision the world through categories such as norms, mores, and folkways. As she suggests, sociology offers her new ways of imagining social relations, allegiances, subjectivities, and futures. Furthermore, she implies that her increasing sense of self-awareness does not refer only to her personal world but is instead universal knowledge, an "awareness of and a feeling for the larger world beyond the familiar pattern" (132).

To become the kind of expert who could compete with the sociologist, Wong had to adapt the forms of authority available to Chinese American women. The scene in which Jade Snow refers to her employers by "type rather than name," describing them as "the horsy family," "the apartment-house family," "the political couple," and "the bridge playing group," exemplifies Wong's fantasy of a Chinese American female expert. After positioning her job as domestic live-in help as the consequence of sexism and global events, she also suggests that it ironically becomes an opportunity to study the daily rituals and customs of white middle-class Americans. Her sociological training prepares her to figure herself as an object ("The small, lone female Jade Snow must have been merely another kitchen fixture for they never recognized her," 106) as a means of opening a space in which she is not a subordinate, but rather a privileged observer and analyst. Composed into a view, the space of a white American home is made available for Jade Snow to observe and define. As part of this process, she compares their households to the "high standards," "Confucian decorum," and "Christian ideals" of the Wong household and finds them wanting (106). It is here that we see most clearly how Wong negotiates sociology's authority and methods. By adapting its formal conventions and claims to speak for her, she constructs a sphere that is different from, even as it accompanies, the reproduction of scientific authority.

By producing a form of domestic expertise, Wong also displaces the head of the household as the dominant postwar protagonist. As Leti Volpp notes, "The paradigmatic citizen has been constructed in dominant memory both as the head of the domestic household and through whiteness. Histories that focus on the citizenship of white women or the citizenship of Asian American men tell only a partial story."[36] Warning against analyses of race unmediated by gender and analyses of gender unmediated by race, Volpp contends that focusing on Chinese women puts into question the way in which Chinese exclusion, as the first race-based immigration exclusion policy, is generally understood as beginning with the ten-year suspension of immigration for Chinese laborers. Such positions, however, do not take into account legislation such as the Page Law of 1875, which targeted prostitutes from countries seen as "Oriental" and effectively banned Chinese female immigration. By proposing the artist–entrepreneur as the paradigmatic postwar protagonist, Wong displaces the postwar emphasis on the Asian American veteran and middle-class family man.

At first glance, Jade Snow's decision to "put aside an earlier Americanized dream of a husband, a home, a garden, a dog, and children" and to pursue a career in social service might be read as a generic rejection of fifties domesticity and embrace of liberal citizenship (132–33). But Wong's decision to depart from this trajectory suggests that her pottery work and writing have become, in her mind, oppositional practices that are defined through their distance from the dominant national narrative. Even as Wong invests in a progress narrative that might be said to be the complement of cold war U.S. ascendancy, she also deploys that notion of progress as a means to investigate the contradictions of race and gender within the liberal democratic discourse of Asian American citizenship.

Wong's text repeatedly calls attention to the transformative effects of Jade Snow's borrowings from sociological methods and authority. But it also points toward the limits of sociology, expressing skepticism of "some of the so-called scientific reasoning expounded in the sociology class, where heredity and environment were assigned all the responsibility for personal success and failure" (131). By insisting that sociology is insufficiently attentive to the complexity of the individual, Wong expresses a desire for an analytical framework that can resist such essentialism. Behind Wong's representation of the possibilities of art is a critique of sociology's explanatory power. In pointing out the deficiencies of sociological theorizing, Wong revises the dominant view of sociology as a knowledge producer of scientific "truth," indicating instead how sociology invests in and reinscribes essentialist discourses about Chinese Americans. In remembering how the image of the Chinese prostitute and the coolie inspired and assisted cultural and political arguments for racial exclusion in the United States, Wong calls for representations of Chinese Americans that resist such essentialism and instead emphasize creativity and complexity. As she sees it, art is an alternative form of knowledge production to sociology. According to Wong, her pottery drew inspiration from others but was "nevertheless her own creation, a combination of the clay she chose, the form she achieved, and the glazes she used. They . . . were physical remembrances of certain personal moments in time which could never be considered lost so long as the pottery was not broken beyond repair" (178).

Wong's pottery is an attempt to create an alternative to the constraints of sociological definitions that sought to classify her as a product of biological race and her environment. To envision a future without such constraints, she insists upon the importance of understanding the conditions under which she is being imagined and interpreted. Wong's text does not pursue more positive representations, but rather investigates what it means to be defined as a "redeemable" racial group rather than a "problem" or "solution" (258).

The historical moment that *Fifth Chinese Daughter* chronicles has been understood primarily through heroic narratives of progress that emphasize U.S. postwar ascendancy, U.S. wartime immigration reforms, and Asian American family formation. By appropriating sociology's sanctioned scientific language and object-making practices, Wong puts into question the transformation of Asian Americans from foreign invaders to potential citizens. In proposing the artist–entrepreneur as an alternative to the Asian American veteran, Wong reveals how a postwar discourse of Asian American citizenship assists state efforts to universalize a male-centered culture through immigration reforms, challenges charges by Communist nations that the United States is a racist nation, and fosters capitalist relations of production in Asia.

By identifying the changing status of Asian Americans as part of a postwar global shift, Wong puts into question the dominant liberal narrative that held that Asian Americans could be racially "redeemed" as culturally assimilable subjects in contrast to black Americans. Through her figure of the artist–entrepreneur, Wong redefines the U.S.-trained Asian-oriented technocrat that Luce envisioned at the center of "The American Century" and suggests the need to frame the postwar "Oriental problem" as a process of comparative racialization that is also shaped by specific conceptions of Asians as racial and sexual others. What enables Wong to revise the figuration of Chinese women as complements to and emblems of a progressive narrative of Asian American citizenship is her engagement with academic sociology.

As Vijay Prashad observes, the figure of the student of color in the narrative of U.S. capitalist progress has more recently and explicitly been co-opted by Fortune 500 companies in the 2001 affirmative action legal brief that details their stated desire to hire managers of color who are equipped with "cross cultural experience and understanding" gained from their experience with "racially and ethnically diverse populations" in the United States.

So imagined, this set of managers of color has the U.S. training that would enable them to handle the demands of the global marketplace and increasing diversity in the Unitd States as well as to serve racially and ethnically diverse communities abroad. Noting this institutional and ideological web, Prashad concludes, "The desire for the student of color to become the comprador for global capital is now established."[37]

Fifth Chinese Daughter proposes a different configuration of the convergence between liberal multiculturalism and the university than the one that Prashad outlines in his more contemporary analysis. Through a series of anecdotes about how she learns to use her training, Wong registers the specific terms of her incorporation into Mills College as domestic help, but frames it as her introduction to a Chinese diaspora and transpacific imaginary. She notes that the kitchen staff was "entirely Chinese" and that many were descendants of earlier employees who had worked for the college founders. In addition, her fellow students include a "native of China," a granddaughter of Sun Yat-sen, the founder of the Republic of China; a Chinese from Honolulu; a Japanese from Tokyo; and an American girl from the state of Washington. Using Wong's narrative to open up questions of agency in the Fortune 500 brief can, I believe, provide us with a nuanced account of the figure of the artist–entrepreneur as it takes shape at the crossroads of race riots in U.S. cities, Luce's powerful vision of a globally oriented technocracy, and notions of Asian American progress and citizenship.

Coda

The Tutelary Byways of Global Uplift

The production of a racialized professional class is a story of U.S. international ascendancy and racial reform from the 1940s and 1950s that is retold even today. Tracing the pedagogical impulses, racial comparisons, and tutelary frameworks used to explain programs of racial reform and neocolonialism during and after World War II allows us to consider the contemporary discourses of Americanization and economic development that the promotion of professionals of color helps to explain and make legitimate. Chapter 4 connects U.S. conceptualizations of Asia as the stage for postwar economic expansion to an emerging class of U.S.-trained experts that could convey a progressive image of the United States. Illuminating this ideological web, I hope, will help us to understand how and why notions of skilled labor, outsourcing, and subcontracting and sites such as call centers have become inseparable from contemporary conceptualizations of nations such as India and the Philippines.

A contemporary illustration of the production of a globally oriented and mobile class of U.S.-trained professionals can be found in the John Pickle Company (JPC) human trafficking case.[1] JPC, a manufacturer of oil industry equipment, imported fifty-three skilled Indian laborers, including welders, engineers, fitters, cooks, and electricians, to its main plant in Tulsa, Oklahoma, in October 2001. Selected by a Mumbai-based labor-recruiting firm, these professionals met personally with John Nash Pickle, the company's founder, who promised them high wages, health insurance, good accommodations, a minimum of two-year contracts, and the means to obtain green cards that would enable them to bring their families to the United States. Upon their arrival in the United States, however, they were paid miniscule wages and confined to cramped housing in the Tulsa plant. The U.S. media denounced JPC's treatment of workers as a form of slavery, highlighting the lower pay they received for the same labor as American workers, confiscation of their passports, intimidation of workers, false imprisonment, and fraudulent promises regarding living and work conditions. As a result of the Equal Employment Opportunity Commission's prosecution of JPC on charges of national-origins discrimination and human trafficking, Pickle closed the Tulsa plant in 2002 and was ordered by a federal court to pay a $1.3 million settlement to the fifty-three laborers in May 2006. As a result of this decision, the Pickle case is widely viewed as a legal victory for foreign workers in the United States.

But what is curious in this story are the ideological linkages between a historic U.S. colonial framework of tutelary assimilation and Pickle's view of Indian laborers, exemplified by JPC's conceptualization of the imported workers as objects of reform in what the Mumbai-based labor recruiter called the "JPC culture" and what Pickle himself called the "American way." What has prevented us from connecting JPC's move to open an "overseas factory" with cheap labor on "American soil" (and not abroad) to these broader and historic discourses of progress and civilization are U.S. media representations of the case as an "American" story of individual malfeasance and capitalist greed as well an isolated example of globalization gone awry. For example, the National Public Radio (NPR) program "This American Life" included the case in a series of stories about the "unintended consequences of market forces" as an example of how businessmen "just push things further than others are willing to go."[2] Even as the title of the section devoted to the case, "Cowboys and Indians," situates the Indian laborers in the historic role of Native Americans and invites a nation-centered reading of the case. "This American Life" also treats the arrival of the Indian workers on U.S. soil as the story's beginning in a way that classifies it as an archetypal and linear American immigrant narrative. Other media reports depict the Pickle case as "the American Dream transformed into a workplace nightmare," but also confine its implications to U.S. national borders and limit the contexts in which it might be read. By defining JPC's "problem" only in terms of its

violation of American labor standards, such accounts also imply that it has
been resolved through U.S. legal reform, culminating in the 2006 federal
court decision.[3]

What existing accounts of the Pickle case either minimize or forget is
that JPC had previously opened a factory in Kuwait and brought two groups
of trainees, a total of twenty-seven workers from India, Pakistan, Bangla-
desh, and the Philippines selected by a recruiting firm, for a two-month training period in Tulsa before sending them to work in the Kuwait operations.
Recovering the Kuwait factory as part of JPC's conceptualization of imported
labor provides an opportunity to study the ways that it is inspired by larger,
historic discourses of racial reform, economic mobility, and civilization.

Through such descriptions of the first group of workers imported to Tulsa
as having "an almost insatiable appetite for learning" and also of JPC's presen-
tation of "Certificates of Accomplishments" to the second group at a farewell
dinner before their departure for Kuwait, JPC's corporate literature depicts
the training program as offering a civilized outlet, moral direction, and global
perspective to its primitive foreign subjects.[4] The Tulsa factory, in this sense,
serves as a staging ground for a longer trajectory of U.S.-sponsored economic
uplift for India and not as a local educational initiative or vocational program. Taking the position of a benevolent American educator, Pickle defines
his role and that of the United States in terms of the cultivation of raw Asian
potential for the economic reform of India, through the social and financial
capital that the laborers will bring back, and an America that is overly regu-
lated by the U.S. government. To be sure, Pickle saw his recruitment of the
Indian laborers, whom he called the "India boys," as a means of offering them
training that would render them eligible to compete in the global market.[5]

In his study of labor practices in the new global economy, reporter John
Bowe suggests that Pickle was not a rogue capitalist so much as someone who
believed that he was helping Indian laborers by hiring them to work under
conditions that he saw as invariably better than those that existed in India.[6]
But reducing the Pickle case to a question of Pickle's intentions and morals
seems limiting in the sense that it does not provide a way to consider the
Indian laborers as social actors, rather than only as objects in the JPC work
program and subsequent legal cases.

At times, the Indian professionals seem to reinforce limited readings of
the case as an American immigrant story. In interviews, they construct themselves and other members of the group as potential U.S. immigrants who gave
up good jobs in India to accept positions at JPC that offered them the possibility of settling in the United States with their families. One such example

is Uday Dattatray Ludbe, who foregrounds the stark contrast between JPC's promises to help workers obtain U.S. green cards and the harsh conditions imposed on them at the Tulsa plant. But in emphasizing their status as skilled professionals with many years of work experience, Ludbe and the other workers also point to their familiarity with different models of professionalization and migration and also to the way in which Pickle's training program aimed to prepare them for global export. Several of them, for example, had been previously employed in the United States and Saudi Arabia. Presenting themselves as multiple migrants and professionalized subjects enables them to contest Pickle's stereotypical perception of Indians as a homogenous Third World nation. It also complicates their positioning in U.S. nationalist narratives as foreigners who must be incorporated as U.S. immigrants through U.S. legal intervention. Highlighting the tenuousness of their self-representations has, I hope, underscored the power and flexibility of the U.S. models of professionalization that I have examined in this book.

Acknowledgments

I can scarcely name everyone who has offered me assistance and dialogue, but those who must be mentioned include Rod Ferguson, who opened bold avenues for thinking about a literary critique of canonical sociology and offered invaluable feedback and encouragement; Adria Imada, whose brilliant insights and exemplary collegiality made writing and revising a true pleasure; and Eric Reyes, Susette Min, and Sanda Lwin, whose ideas, interests, and keen readings are everywhere in the book. Many others offered thoughtful advice, clarification, humor, and perspective: Victor Bascara, Oscar Campomanes, Matt Christensen, David Eng, Nicole Fleetwood, Grace Kyungwon Hong, Jodi Melamed, and Delfin L. Tolentino. Heike Raphael-Hernandez and Shannon Steen provided constructive comments on an earlier version of chapter 4. I thank George Lipsitz for generously inviting me to talk with students at the University of California–Santa Cruz, which enabled me to develop parts of the Introduction. None of the people mentioned here should bear responsibility for the final book, but each one has my thanks.

At Brown University, Nancy Armstrong, Daniel Kim, and Leonard Tennenhouse provided intellectual guidance that felt, at once, rigorous, exciting, and spacious. Bob Lee and Susan Smulyan introduced me to the field of American studies. I'm grateful to have had such an inspiring graduate student cohort, including Nate Angell, Laura Briggs, Nick Daly, Jennifer Jang, and Beth Kling. Following graduate school, I had the chance to participate in a lively

Asian American women's academic writing group based in New York, and hearty thanks go to Evelyn Ch'ien, Shirley J. Lim, Mary Lui, Sanda Lwin, Sandhya Shukla, and Lisa Yun. The Consortium for Minority Scholars program provided support for this book by way of a postdoctoral fellowship at Vassar College, and I thank Heesok Chang and Eileen Leonard for my time there. I thank Jack Tchen at New York University, Gary Okihiro at Columbia University, and Rosanne Rocher at the University of Pennsylvania for inviting me to teach Asian American literature and Filipino American studies courses while I was completing my dissertation. The *New York Times* Web site provided me with a flexible and hospitable workplace, and I am grateful to many colleagues there, especially Colby Devitt, Bernard Gwertzman, Jed Miller, Elizabeth Osder, and Justin Peacock.

At the University of Oregon, I thank my faculty mentor and friend Shari Huhndorf for the high standards of intellectual and professional integrity she has set. I have benefited enormously from the wisdom and support of Karen Ford, Anthony Foy, Lynn Fujiwara, Linda Kintz, David Li, Fabienne Moore, Steve Morizumi, Jenifer Presto, Dan Rosenberg, Dick Stein, Martin Summers, and David Vásquez. I owe much gratitude to Marilyn Reid and Susan Dickens for the English Department's smooth functioning. Thanks also to the librarians and staff at the University of Oregon's Knight Library for help with databases, borrowing networks, and other essential resources. The Bibliothèque Nationale de France–François Mitterrand provided me with valuable distance, silent camaraderie, and a sleek mise-en-scène for my manuscript revisions.

I am lucky to have had the opportunity to work with an editor as supportive, insightful, and ethical as Richard Morrison. Profound thanks to the anonymous reviewers for pushing me to think more precisely and responsively and for pointing me in fruitful directions. This book is immeasurably better because of the editorial expertise and technical savoir-faire of the University of Minnesota Press staff.

I am forever grateful to Roger Tolentino, J. V. Tolentino, and Victoria Estrada and thank them for their patience and important presence in my life. Finally, I thank Timur Friedman, whose extraordinary creativity, intelligence, and love have made all the difference.

Notes

Introduction

1. William S. Bryan, ed., *Our Islands and Their Peoples: As Seen with Camera and Pencil* (St. Louis, Mo.: N. D. Thompson Publishing Company, 1899). The phrase "subjects of interest" refers to ways in which sociologists have historically constructed communities of color as objects of study as well as to the allure of sociology as an authoritative discourse that enabled racialized subjects to engage this relationship. This phrase critically expresses the processes of objectification and discourses of professionalization through which we can apprehend the linkages between practices of prewar U.S. colonialism and post–World War II neocolonialism across historical periods and geographic areas. In contrast to "person of interest," the phrase that police use to refer to individual suspects in criminal investigations, "subjects of interest" denotes a climate of progressive and compassionate concern rather than direct and disciplinary surveillance.

2. Bryan, *Our Islands and Their Peoples*, 7.

3. As Wheeler writes, "Be it ours to lift them from the low estate of unwilling subjects to the high plane of independent citizenship, to extend to them the knowledge of our beneficent institutions, and to help them onward and upward to the realization of the loftiest ideals of perfection in human government and the universal happiness of mankind." Bryan, *Our Islands and Their Peoples*, 7.

4. On the analogy of tribes, see Lanny Thompson, "Representation and Rule in the Imperial Archipelago: Cuba, Puerto Rico, Hawaii, and the Philippines under U.S. Dominion after 1898," *American Studies Asia* 1, no. 1 (2002): 3–35, 25–30.

5. As Paul Kramer explains the inclusionary logic of U.S. colonial state-building in the Philippines during and after the Philippine-American War, which tends to focus on the relationship between Filipinos and white Americans: "The new political

configuration necessitated a new racial formation to organize and legitimate it. . . . What was needed was a racial formation that could somehow persuade its Filipino participants that they were 'brothers' and not 'serfs' and simultaneously explain to them why they were unready for the rigors and responsibilities of self-government" (161). Paul A. Kramer, *The Blood of Government: Race, Empire, the United States, and the Philippines* (Chapel Hill: University of North Carolina Press, 2006).

6. See Bienvenido Santos, "Scent of Apples," in *Scent of Apples* (Seattle: University of Washington Press, 1997), 21–29. For an insightful reading and fuller treatment of "Scent of Apples," see Victor Bascara's "Up from Benevolent Assimilation: At Home with the Manongs of Bienvenido Santos," *MELUS* 29, no. 1 (spring 2004): 61–78.

7. For an account of the impact of sociological studies on Filipino racialization, see Mae M. Ngai, *Impossible Subjects: Illegal Aliens and the Making of Modern America* (Princeton, N.J.: Princeton University Press, 2004), 109–16. As Ngai notes, a common theme in sociological literature in the 1930s was that the "abnormal sex ratio among Filipinos in the United States had led to 'social and psychological maladjustment,' which in turn led to 'moral problems.' Constantly on the move, following the harvest season, these itinerant young single men lacked both family life and a stable community. More than anything, it was argued, they lacked moral supervision" (111).

8. For an example of how sociologists framed race mixing between Filipinos and white women and racial conflict between Filipinos and whites as the outcomes of Filipino deviation from heterosexual relations and family norms, see Donald Elliot Anthony, "Filipino Labor in Central California," *Sociology and Social Research* 16, no. 3 (January–February 1932): 149–56.

9. As Roderick Ferguson notes, African American intellectuals had to present their own histories as "ones emptied of formations that contradict universality. . . . During periods of segregation and industrialization, African American sociologists were incapable of claiming the illusory universality fostered by canonical sociology. Black sociologists such as St. Claire Drake, Horace Cayton, and E. Franklin Frazier operated within a historical moment that constructed the black body as the antithesis of the rationality and universality of Western epistemology and American citizenship. Whereas the bodies of canonical, i.e., white, sociologists were unmarked by particularities of gender, sexuality, class, and race, the bodies of black sociologists were the signs of racial differences that placed the rationality of African American sociologists into question." See Roderick A. Ferguson, *Aberrations in Black: Toward a Queer of Color Critique* (Minneapolis: University of Minnesota Press, 2004), 22.

10. As Henry Yu observes, "Asian Americans, like African Americans and other intellectuals of color in the United States, did not (and in many ways still do not) have the freedom of possibilities that white scholars enjoyed." See Henry Yu, "On a Stage Built by Others: Creating an Intellectual History of Asian America," *Amerasia Journal* 26, no. 1 (2000): 141–61, 150. Vijay Prashad also situates the institutionalization of the professional of color as emerging in a materialist account of U.S. global ascendancy during the cold war, but locates the origins of comparative race scholarship in the Bandung conference and Richard Wright's book *The Color Curtain*. See Vijay Prashad, "Foreword: Bandung Is Done: Passages in AfroAsian Epistemology," in *AfroAsian Encounters: Culture, History, Politics*, eds. Heike Raphael Hernandez and Shannon M. Steen (New York: New York University Press, 2006).

11. Robert Park writes, "The Japanese bears in his features a distinctive racial hallmark . . . a racial uniform that classifies him." See Robert E. Park, *Race and Culture* (Glencoe, Ill.: The Free Press, 1950), 208–9.

12. Writing against the immigrant's arrival in America as the definitive point of reference for Asian American histories, Okihiro promotes a transnational framework based on the structuring presence of Orientalist perceptions of Asians in European historical consciousness. See Gary Y. Okihiro, *Margins and Mainstreams* (Seattle: University of Washington, 1994).

13. Prashad, "Foreword: Bandung Is Done," xv.

14. Oscar V. Campomanes, "The New Empire's Forgetful and Forgotten Citizens," *Critical Mass: A Journal of Asian American Cultural Criticism* 2, no. 2 (spring 1995): 145–200, 147.

15. Vicente Rafael, "White Love: Surveillance and Nationalist Resistance in the U.S. Colonization in the Philippines," in *Cultures of United States Imperialism*, eds. Amy Kaplan and Donald E. Pease (Durham, N.C.: Duke University Press, 1993), 186–87.

16. The role of the white liberal in American race relations was the subject of a 1964 round-table discussion titled "Liberalism and the Negro," moderated by Norman Podheretz, with James Baldwin, Nathan Glazer, Sidney Hook, and Gunnar Myrdal. An edited transcript of the discussion was later published in *Commentary* 37 (March 1964).

17. Cited in Louise Michele Newman, *White Women's Rights: The Racial Origins of American Feminism in the United States* (New York and Oxford, UK: Oxford University Press, 1999), 15.

18. Kramer, *The Blood of Government*, 110.

19. See Julian Go, *The American Colonial State in the Philippines: Global Perspectives*, eds. Julian Go and Anne L. Foster (Durham, N.C.: Duke University Press, 2003), 24, 151.

20. For an account of the model minority myth and discourse as a form of assimilation, see David Palumbo Liu, *Asian/American: Historical Crossings of a Racial Frontier* (Palo Alto, Calif.: Stanford University Press, 1999), 395–400. Also, for an alternative to figurations of the Asian American model minority as a product of 1960s social movements and black pathologization, see Robert Lee's account of the cold war origins of the model minority myth. Robert G. Lee, *Orientals: Asian Americans in American Popular Cultures* (Philadelphia, Pa.: Temple University Press, 1999), 145–79. For an account of the cultural production of the Asian American as model minority and a critical component of U.S. geopolitics, see Colleen Lye, *America's Asia: Racial Form and American Literature, 1893–1945* (Princeton, N.J.: Princeton University Press, 2005), 10–11.

21. James Kyung-Jin Lee, *Urban Triage: Race and the Fictions of Multiculturalism* (Minneapolis: University of Minnesota Press, 2004), 101.

22. Kandice Chuh proposes to use subjectlessness as a means of creating a conceptual space that prioritizes difference by highlighting the "discursive constructedness of subjectivity" and in so doing sounding the limits of the liberatory possibilities of the achievement of subjectivity. A subject, Chuh points out, "only becomes recognizable and can act as such by conforming to certain regulatory matrices. In that sense, a

subject is always also an epistemological object" (9). Kandice Chuh, *Imagine Otherwise: On Asian American Cultural Politics* (Durham, N.C.: Duke University Press, 2003).

23. A key consequence of the discourse of the bad subject, Viet Nguyen notes, is its "inability to account for its own practices of interpellation—the practice of hailing Asian Americans, but also hailing them to behave in particular ways as Asian American. . . . Asian American intellectuals who see themselves as bad subjects that resist dominant society's interpellation into a race and class stratified society may also seek to interpellate others." Viet Thanh Nguyen, *Race and Resistance in Asian America* (New York: Oxford University Press, 2002), 150.

24. Henry Yu, "On a Stage Set by Others: Creating an Intellectual History of Asian Americans," *Amerasia Journal* 26, no. 1 (2000): 141–61.

25. Remarking that scholarship's focus on the metropole has contributed to the production of the Other as an object rather than subject, thus reproducing the "privileged position of the Western, liberal subject" and obstructing the "role of non-Western people as historical subjects in their own right" (60), Mae Ngai notes, for example, "Reorienting our own angle of vision to the transnational might, then, enable a shift from a methodology that emphasizes the production of hegemonic discourses to one that seeks to understand contact, translation, exchange, negotiation, conflict, and other dynamics that attend the constitution of social relationships across cultural and national borders" (60). Mae M. Ngai, "Transnationalism and the Transformation of the 'Other,'" *American Quarterly* 57, no. 1 (March 2005): 59–65.

26. See, for example, Richard H. Pells, *The Liberal Mind in a Conservative Age: American Intellectuals in the 1940s and 1950s* (Middletown, Conn.: Wesleyan University Press, 1989); Thomas Hill Schaub, *American Fiction in the Cold War* (Madison: University of Wisconsin Press, 1991); and Alan Wald, *The New York Intellectuals: The Rise and Decline of the Anti-Stalinist Left from the 1930s to the 1980s* (Chapel Hill: University of North Carolina Press, 1987).

27. Robin D. G. Kelley, "But a Local Phase of a World Problem: Black History's Global Vision, 1883–1950," *Journal of American History* 86, no. 3 (December 1999): 1045–77, 1077.

28. One famous example of studies that had an impact on wartime policy is anthropologist Ruth Benedict's study of Japan, which became a sourcebook for the U.S. occupation of Japan during the postwar period. In contrast to an idealized democratic American culture, Benedict concluded, "the Japanese were the most alien enemy the United States ever fought in an all-out struggle. In no other war with a major foe had it been necessary to take into account such exceedingly different habits of acting and thinking." Ruth Benedict, *The Chrysanthemum and the Sword* (Boston: Houghton Mifflin, 1946), 1.

29. William Chafe, *The Unfinished Journey since World War II* (New York: Oxford University Press, 2003), 5.

30. For an example of the emphasis on U.S. legal history, particularly the notion of a shift from official Asian exclusion to assimilation in defining the dominant narrative of Asian American progress, see Roger Daniel, *Asian America: Chinese and Japanese in the United States since 1850* (Seattle: University of Washington Press, 1990), 306. For Daniel, the 1952 act marked the full turning of the tide of immigration re-

striction for Asian Americans, a tide that had begun at the federal level with the 1870 naturalization statute and the Chinese Exclusion Act of 1882. In contrast, scholars such as Lucie Cheng and Leti Volpp have illuminated the global and gendered dimensions of immigration restrictions in ways that question the notion of a definitive shift from official Asian exclusion to assimilation. For example, Cheng illuminates the collaboration between Chinese abroad and in the United States to import prostitutes, placing these shifts in global context. See *Labor Immigration under Capitalism*, eds. Lucie Cheng and Edna Bonacich (Berkeley: University of California Press, 1984), 409. See Volpp's suggestion that using the Page Law of 1875, which largely banned Chinese female immigration to the United States, as a historical marker would take into account the gendered form by which the racialized exclusion of Asian immigrants from the U.S. nation-state took place. Leti Volpp, "Divesting Citizenship: On Asian American History and the Loss of Citizenship through Marriage," *UCLA Law Review* 52 (2005). Volpp is also cited in David L. Eng, "Transnational Adoption and Queer Diasporas," *Social Text* 21, no. 3 (Fall 2003): 1–38, 23.

31. Barbara Ehrenreich, *Fear of Falling: The Inner Life of the Middle Classes* (New York: Pantheon Books, 1989), 13. See also Barbara Ehrenreich and John Ehrenreich, "The Professional Managerial Class," in *Between Labor and Capital*, ed. Pat Walker (Boston: South End Press, 1979), 5–45. The Ehrenreichs use this term to explain the predominantly middle-class composition of the left during and in the years after the 1960s.

32. Edward Said, *Orientalism* (1978; New York: Random House, 1979), 10.

33. "It is the educated and trained blacks who are slated to become the new managers of the ghetto," Allen writes, "the administrators of the black colony." See Robert L. Allen, *Black Awakening in Capitalist America: An Analytic History* (1969; Garden City, N.Y.: Doubleday, 1970), 261–62. Quoted in Prashad, xvii.

34. David L. Eng, *Racial Castration: Managing Masculinity in Asian America* (Durham, N.C.: Duke University Press, 2001), 19.

35. "This is not to say," Wiegman states, "that the literary and artistic productions of the historically minoritized should not be retrieved from the sociological approach that has most often accompanied their critical evaluation." See Robyn Wiegman, "Difference and Disciplinarity," in *Aesthetics in a Multicultural Age*, eds. Emory Elliott, Louis Freitas Caton, and Jeffrey Rhyne (New York and London, UK: Oxford University Press, 2002), 139.

1. Sociological Interests, Racial Reform

1. Robert E. Park, "Negro Race Consciousness as Reflected in Race Literature," in *Race and Culture: The Collected Papers of Robert Ezra Park* (New York: Arno Press, 1974), 285.

2. Park, "Negro Race Consciousness as Reflected in Race Literature," 284.

3. My work on liberal narratives of race draws from Thomas Hill Schaub's study of liberalism and cold war American fiction of the 1950s. As Schaub writes, "The word 'liberalism' refers not to a monolithic or univocal event, set of people, or doctrine, but to a moiré of usage, invoking an indeterminate array of connotations, each of which

brings into play other terms and meanings." See Thomas Hill Schaub, *American Fiction in the Cold War* (Madison: University of Wisconsin Press, 1991), 5.

4. Park, "Negro Race Consciousness as Reflected in Race Literature," 285.

5. Ibid.

6. Wright's essay "I Tried to Be a Communist" is often seen as having inaugurated a genre of black cultural history that centers on African American creative struggles with a white U.S. literary and political left. See Richard Wright, "I Tried to Be a Communist," *Atlantic Monthly* 174 (1944): [1] August: 61–70; [2] September: 48–56.

7. I use the word "communist" with a lowercase C to refer to individuals, movements, and ideas that saw themselves as communist generally. "Communist" with a capital C will be used to denote individuals, events, and ideas directly connected to the Third International, founded in 1919 by Soviet Bolsheviks.

8. See, for example, Bill Mullen's characterization of the essay as ushering a new era in which "black Americans struggle to find their artistic and political voice in relationship to the brutalizing tendencies of the white Left." Bill V. Mullen, *Popular Fronts: Chicago and African American Cultural Politics, 1935–1946* (Champaign: University of Illinois Press, 1999), 21. Quoted in Nikhil Singh, "Retracing the Black-Red Thread," *American Literary History* 15, no. 4 (2003): 830–40.

9. My reading of *Native Son* as a novel about the professionalization of black subjects departs from the narratives through which it is usually discussed. In speaking of the novel's proletarian themes, Walter Rideout contends that the "imaginative expansion of the book, the quality which survives both melodrama and didacticism, comes from the relating of the truncated lives of Negroes in the United States to those of all the other 'have nots,' the humiliated and despised, who are goaded on by the American dream and whose tragedy it is to be blocked from the dream's fulfillment." Whereas Rideout emphasizes the novel's interest in depicting the possibility of a united proletariat, I argue that the novel is more interested in thematizing the processes of professionalization imagined for black subjects. Walter B. Rideout, *The Radical Novel in the United States, 1900–1954* (Cambridge, Mass.: Harvard University Press, 1957), 261. Cedric Robinson also emphasizes the book's proletarian themes, but productively connects them to a transnational framework: "Bigger Thomas's character was specific to the historical experience of Blacks in the U.S., but his nature was proletarian, that is world-historical." See Cedric J. Robinson, *Black Marxism: The Making of the Black Radical Tradition* (Chapel Hill: University of North Carolina Press, 2000), 297. My chapter takes a different approach by proposing that Wright positions Bigger Thomas at the crossroads of competing discourses regarding the professionalization of black subjects.

10. Paul Gilroy, "Without the Consolation of Tears: Richard Wright, France, and the Ambivalence of Community," in *The Black Atlantic* (London and New York: Verso, 1993), 146–86, 147.

11. Communist theoreticians, Robin Kelley notes, generally assumed that authentic black folk culture was implicitly revolutionary. Following this logic, antireligious Communists could positively view African American spiritual expressions as referencing the religious past only to point to their Communist present; other Communists read Negro spirituals as live expressions of Communist protest and faith in

deliverance. See Robin D. G. Kelley, *Race Rebels: Culture, Politics, and the Black Working Class* (New York: The Free Press, 1996), 117.

12. St. Clair Drake and Horace R. Clayton, *Black Metropolis: A Study of Negro Life in a Northern City* (1945; Chicago: University of Chicago Press, 1993).

13. Writing against entrenched assumptions that depict Wright's and Ralph Ellison's rejection of the party as simply a shift away from left radicalism into liberalism and literary fame, as some critics have suggested, Nikhil Singh points out that the wartime views of both writers cannot be regarded only as "anticommunist," but also sought to generate an independent black radicalism. Singh, "Retracing the Black-Red Thread," *American Literary History* 15, no. 4 (2003): 830–40.

14. Booker T. Washington, *Up from Slavery* (New York: W. W. Norton & Company, 1996), 52.

15. See, for example, Charles S. Johnson's *Growing Up in the Black Belt* and E. Franklin Frazier's *Negro Youth at the Crossway*, both published around 1940.

16. Oscar Campomanes and Amy Kaplan have argued persuasively that historical accounts that trace U.S. global power and political expansion only to World War II have largely contributed to the erasure of the United States' colonization of the Philippines during the Spanish-American War. See Oscar Campomanes, "The New Empire's Forgetful and Forgotten Citizens: Unrepresentability, Unassimilability in Filipino American Postcolonialities," *Critical Mass: A Journal of Asian American Cultural Criticism* 2, no. 2 (spring 1995): 145–200, and Amy Kaplan, "Left Alone with America: The Absence of Empire in the Study of American Culture," in *Cultures of United States Imperialism*, eds. Amy Kaplan and Donald Pease (Durham, N.C.: Duke University Press, 1993).

17. As Paula Rabinowitz reminds us, there were "abrupt shifts in line among leftists as the Communist Party in the United States (CPUSA) instituted its own version of Stalinism." Paula Rabinowitz, *Labor and Desire: Women's Revolutionary Fiction in Depression America* (Chapel Hill and London: University of North Carolina Press, 1991), 17. For other accounts of the political left in the United States, see Richard Pells, *The Liberal Mind in a Conservative Age: American Intellectuals in the 1940s and 1950s* (Middletown: Wesleyan University Press, 1985). Also, Alan Wald, *The New York Intellectuals: The Rise and Decline of the Anti-Stalinist Left from the 1930s to the 1980s* (Chapel Hill: University of North Carolina Press, 1987).

18. William J. Maxwell, *New Negro, Old Left: African-American Writing and Communism between the Wars* (New York: Columbia University Press, 1999), 70.

19. Maxwell, 7.

20. "How 'Bigger' Was Born" was originally a talk that Wright gave at Columbia University on March 12, 1940, and at the Schomberg Library in Harlem a few weeks later. A shorter version was later published in the *Saturday Review of Literature* issue of June 1, 1940, and also in an even more condensed essay in *Negro Digest* in the fall of 1940. In August 1940, Harper and Brothers published the first complete text as a separate pamphlet of thirty-nine pages and in 1942 added the essay as the introduction to later printings of Wright's novel *Native Son*. This account and textual references for "How 'Bigger' Was Born" are drawn from *Richard Wright: Early Works*, ed. Arnold Rampersad (New York: Library of America, 1991), 851–82.

21. See Fanon's discussion of counter-hegemony and the role of culture in his theory of formation of national consciousness, particularly his theorization of national culture as "contested culture." Frantz Fanon, *The Wretched of the Earth*, trans. Constance Farrington (New York: Penguin, 1967), 206–48.

22. Richard Wright, "Blueprint for Negro Writing," in *African American Literary Theory: A Reader*, ed. Winston Napier (1937; New York and London: New York University, 2000), 45–53, 51. Further references will be cited parenthetically.

23. In his study of nationalism, Benedict Anderson links print culture to the formation of national collective consciousness. As he explains, print capitalism, or the mass distribution of texts, effectively changed the way in which people imagined their relationships to one another and envisioned their place within a nation. While Anderson sees literary production as a condition of national consciousness, he locates the origins of the process through which consciousness is formed in the economic system that produces these texts rather than in fiction. By blurring the distinction between fiction and sociology, Wright suggests a different view: that the formation of collective consciousness, and hence new types of agency and subjectivity, takes place through fiction, not as a result of it. For a critique of Anderson, see Nancy Armstrong and Leonard Tennenhouse, "A Novel Nation; or, How to Rethink Modern England as an Emergent Culture," *Modern Language Quarterly* 54 (1993): 327–44.

24. Wright, "Blueprint for Negro Writing," 51.

25. Arguing against the desirability of "pure particularism," Laclau writes, "If the particularity asserts itself as mere particularity, in a purely differential relation with other particularities, it is sanctioning the status quo in the relation of power between the groups. This is exactly the notion 'separate developments' as formulated in apartheid: only the differential aspect is stressed, while the relations of power on which the latter is based are systematically ignored" (100). Ernesto Laclau, "Universalism, Particularism, and the Question of Identity," in *The Identity in Question*, ed. John Rajchman (New York: Routledge, 1995), 93–108.

26. See Richard Dyer, *White: Essays on Race and Culture* (London: Routledge, 1997), 46.

27. In his study of the constitution of the white working class in the nineteenth century, David R. Roediger remarks that comparisons between African Americans and the Irish stemmed from a number of environmental and historical (rather than biological) factors, including job competition and neighborhood rivalries. But even as he suggests there were "strong signs that the Irish might not fully embrace white supremacy," he proceeds to catalog ways in which the Irish working class appropriated and defended the entitlements and rights associated with whiteness, most often through violence directed at blacks. With the rise in immigration during the 1840s and 1850s, the Irish increasingly began to assert themselves as white rather than Irish, thereby distancing themselves from blacks and other immigrant groups, such as Jews, Eastern Europeans, and Italians (134). See David Roediger, *The Wages of Whiteness: Race and the Making of the American Working Class*, rev. ed. (New York: Verso, 1991), 133–36.

28. Aside from Green, other black Americans are positioned in varying degrees of identification and difference from Bigger Thomas, marking out various paths avail-

able to him as a black man in the thirties. For example, Bigger's mother, with her tired resignation to Jim Crow laws, longing for middle-class domesticity, and pleas for Christian mercy, represents the suffering black subject begging for recognition of black humanity that Wright rejects in his essay on African American writing.

29. Also, Saidiya Hartman argues that the transition from chattel slavery to Reconstruction generated a genre of literature directed toward instructing freed blacks on the "ways of white folks" in order to improve interactions between blacks and whites. Saidiya V. Hartman, *Scenes of Subjection: Terror, Slavery, and Self-Making in Nineteenth Century America* (New York: Oxford University Press, 1997). In *Native Son*, we see a different dynamic in which white Americans are being encouraged to learn about black culture as part of a process of national reform and the repudiation of racial bigotry. In both cases, however, racial knowledge is posited as a crucial factor in narratives of social progress and the nation's democratic well-being.

2. Americanization as Black Professionalization

1. Gunnar Myrdal, *An American Dilemma: The Negro Problem and Modern Democracy* (New York and London: Harper & Brothers Publishers, 1944).

2. Ralph Ellison, for example, famously denounced Myrdal's reinforcement of the notion that "Negroes should desire nothing better than what whites consider highest." Noting the study's definition of principles of equality and liberty as natural to white Americans, Ellison challenged its implication that African Americans are neither full nor "natural" Americans and alternatively called for the efforts of African Americans and white Americans in the "creation of a democracy in which the Negro will be free to define himself for what he is and within the large framework of that democracy" (4). Ralph Ellison, "An American Dilemma: A Review," in *Shadow and Act* (1944; New York: Vintage Books, 1995), 303–17.

3. Walter Jackson, *Gunnar Myrdal and America's Conscience* (Chapel Hill: University of North Carolina Press, 1990), 177.

4. Jackson, *Gunnar Myrdal and America's Conscience*, 177.

5. Exceptions to this treatment are Roderick A. Ferguson's *Aberrations in Black* (Minneapolis: University of Minnesota Press, 2003); also see Jodi Melamed's positioning of Myrdal in relation to U.S. racial liberalism and neocolonialism in "W. E. B. Du Bois's UnAmerican End," *African American Review* 40, no. 3 (2006): 533–50, 534, 536–38.

6. "Perhaps the War can this time be won even without the colored people's confidence," writes Myrdal. "But the absence of their full cooperation, and still more their obstructive activities, will be tremendously costly in time, men, and materials. Caste is becoming an expensive luxury of white men" (1016).

7. Melamed, "W. E. B. Du Bois's UnAmerican End," 534.

8. Myrdal, *An American Dilemma*, 1022–24.

9. Jackson, *Gunnar Myrdal and America's Conscience*, 173.

10. Stephen Steinberg, *Turning Back: The Retreat from Racial Justice in American Thought and Policy* (Boston: Beacon Press, 1995), 49.

11. Matthew Jacobson, *Whiteness of a Different Color: European Immigrants and the Alchemy of Race* (Cambridge, Mass.: Harvard University Press, 1999), 265.

12. Jackson, *Gunnar Myrdal and America's Conscience*, 293.

13. Robin D. G. Kelley and Earl Lewis, eds., *We Changed the World: African Americans, 1945–1970* (New York: Oxford University Press, 1997). From a different angle, Daryl Michael Scott contests the connection that is frequently evoked between Myrdal and *Brown v. Board*. For Scott, "the road to Brown and integration was laid by the liberal pluralist's approach to race relations, not Gunnar Myrdal's evocation of the American creed." Daryl Michael Scott, "Postwar Pluralism, *Brown v. Board of Education*, and the Origins of Multicultural Education," *Journal of American History* 91, no. 1 (June 2004): 69–82.

14. Indeed, Walter Jackson even notes that Myrdal died on the day of the thirty-third anniversary of the *Brown v. Board* decision, May 17, 1987 (Jackson, 367).

15. Myrdal offers this definition of the American Creed: "Americans of all national origins, classes, regions, creeds, and colors, have something in common: a social ethos, a political creed. It is difficult to avoid the judgment that this American Creed is the cement in the structure of this great and disparate nation" (*An American Dilemma*, 3).

16. On U.S. manifest destiny, see *An American Dilemma*, 66.

17. Roderick Ferguson emphasizes Baker's theorization of chattel slavery as positing capitalism as a mechanism that will advance the civilizing process for African Americans. See Ferguson, *Aberrations in Black*, 89. As Ferguson argues, "Situating efforts to civilize African Americans within an economy constituted by the productive needs of chattel slavery, Baker, in fact, identifies the capitalist relations of production as the mode through which African Americans are civilized, as the key that can release blacks from their 'wild' and 'savage' habits."

18. Paul A. Kramer, *The Blood of Government: Race, the Philippines, and U.S. Empire* (Chapel Hill: University of North Carolina Press, 2006), 392.

19. Kramer, *The Blood of Government*, 86.

20. As David Southern notes, "Owing to the international rising tide of colored peoples, the Soviets, Myrdal predicted, would woo the nonwhite nations of the world with a flood of egalitarian propaganda." David W. Southern, *Gunnar Myrdal and Black-White Relations: The Use and Abuse of an American Dilemma, 1944–1969* (Baton Rouge: Louisiana State University, 1987), 50.

21. Myrdal generated a discourse of African American pathology through numerous references to African American cultural distinctiveness, including the "type of religious experience they seek, the news they read, the art they create, and the disorganization and rivalry manifested in their families and social gatherings" (783).

22. Oliver Cox offers a trenchant critique of Myrdal's assumption that middle-class formation would solve racism. Especially incensed by Myrdal's contention that upper-class whites were less racist to blacks than white workers, Cox countered that these elites used only tactics of racial domination that were viewed as more respectable in ways that also rendered them more powerful. Oliver C. Cox, *Caste, Class and Race* (1948; New York: Monthly Review Press, 1970).

23. See Robert E. Park and Ernest W. Burgess, *Introduction to the Science of Sociology*, 3rd ed. (Chicago: University of Chicago Press, 1969), 140. Also see Daniel Y.

Kim's discussion of Park's essay on temperament in *Writing Manhood in Black and Yellow: Ralph Ellison, Frank Chin, and the Literary Politics of Identity* (Palo Alto, Calif.: Stanford University Press, 2005), 71–81.

24. Herbert Aptheker, *The Negro People in America* (New York: International Publishers, 1946), 261.

25. Doxey Wilkerson, introduction to *The Negro People in America* (New York: International Publishers, 1946), 258.

26. See Jackson, 258.

27. See C. L. R. James, "Abyssinia and the Imperialists," in *The C. L. R. James Reader,* ed. Anna Grimshaw (Oxford, UK: Blackwell Publishers, 1993), 63. My reading of Myrdal's national exceptionalism expands on Roderick Ferguson's analysis of James, which identifies the inferiorization of blacks as intrinsic to capital's structure. See Ferguson, *Aberrations in Black*, 96.

28. Jackson, *Gunnar Myrdal and America's Conscience*, 260.

29. See Victor Bascara on the colonial classroom as a "liminal institution" between older styles of empire and emerging forms of imperialism. Victor Bascara, *Model Minority Imperialism* (Minneapolis: University of Minnesota Press, 2007), 84.

30. Myrdal, *An American Dilemma*, 893.

31. Ibid., 1417.

32. As Jackson sums up, "No longer a strong power in the nation's politics, the South was itself one of the nation's economic and cultural problems. The North had the means to compel southern compliance and would do so through Congress, the courts, and presidential action. Myrdal bluntly declared that 'it is crucially important . . . that the northern states take on the assignment of planning' and use their power to 'reform the South's caste system.'" Jackson, *Gunnar Myrdal and America's Conscience*, 177.

33. Kramer, *The Blood of Government: Race, the Philippines, and U.S. Empire*, 169. Kramer is quoting from Adeline Knapp, "A Notable Educational Experiment," in *Log of the "Thomas,"* ed. Ronald P. Gleason, from section dated July 23 to August 21, 1991, 1901. Published in 1901, n.p.

34. For Myrdal, education and urbanization are forces that will assist blacks in losing their "distinctive cultural traits and take over the dominant American patterns." Myrdal, *An American Dilemma*, 227.

35. Ibid., 1022–23.

36. Glenn Anthony May, *Social Engineering in the Philippines: The Aims, Execution, and Impact of American Colonial Policy, 1900–1913* (Westport, Conn., and London: Greenwood Press, 1980), xvii. See May's important framing of social engineering as historically linked to the implementation of colonial policy and systematic rule by almost all modern colonial powers, including the efforts of British policymakers of the nineteenth century to reorganize the judicial system and reform the tax system in the colony of India. I disagree with May's claims, however, that the U.S. effort to change the Philippines was entirely "unique" and not self-serving.

37. Speech by Albert Beveridge before the U.S. Senate, 9 January 1900, 56th Congress, 1st session, Congressional Record 33, pt. 1 (1899–1900). Quoted in Kramer, *The Blood of Government: Race, the Philippines, and U.S. Empire*, 2.

38. For more on Myrdal's confidence in social science as the agent of social progress and institutional reform, see *An American Dilemma*, 1024.

39. Myrdal, *An American Dilemma*, xv, 1023.

3. Training for the American Century

1. Henry R. Luce, "The American Century," *Diplomatic History* 23, no. 2 (spring 1999): 170; further references are to this reprint, and page numbers will be cited in parentheses in the text.

2. Here, I take up Oscar Campomanes's shifting use of the terms Filipino, Filipino American, and U.S. Filipino to highlight the ways in which they inhabit and produce contradictions, redundancies, and varying meanings. See Oscar V. Campomanes, "The New Empire's Forgetful and Forgotten Citizens: Unrepresentability and Unassimilability in Filipino-American Postcolonialities," *Critical Mass: A Journal of Asian American Cultural Criticism* 2, no. 2 (spring 1995): 150.

3. See Oscar V. Campomanes, "1898 and the Nature of the New Empire," *Radical History Review* 73 (winter 1999): 135. Mae M. Ngai also points to the visibility of Filipinos as a race problem during the early part of the twentieth century and the United States' "return" following World War II, and to the invisibility of benevolent assimilation and colonialism in the Philippines with the cultural impact, if limited numerical "success," of the official repatriation program for Filipino workers. See Mae M. Ngai, *Impossible Subjects: Illegal Aliens and the Making of Modern America* (Princeton, N.J., and Oxford, UK: Princeton University Press, 2004), 120–26.

4. Ngai, *Impossible Subjects: Illegal Aliens and the Making of Modern America*, 103.

5. For an insightful discussion of how writings on Filipino *manongs* narrate the transition from U.S. territorial colonialism to an ungrounded neocolonial empire, see Victor Bascara, "Up from Benevolent Assimilation: At Home with the Manongs of Bienvenido Santos," *MELUS* 29 (spring 2004): 61–79.

6. Charles Hilliard, *The Cross, the Sword, and the Dollar* (New York: North River Press, 1951), 64–74.

7. William Appleman Williams, 1959, *The Tragedy of American Diplomacy* (New York and London: W. W. Norton, 1988), 20. For a discussion of Williams's observation of the elision of U.S. imperialism in dominant U.S. historiography, see Amy Kaplan, "Left Alone with America: The Absence of Empire in the Study of U.S. Culture," in *Cultures of U.S. Imperialism*, eds. Amy Kaplan and Donald E. Pease (Durham, N.C., and London, UK: Duke University Press, 1993), 3–21.

8. Melani McAlister, *Epic Encounters: Culture, Media, and U.S. Interests in the Middle East, 1945–2000* (Berkeley, Calif., and London, UK: University of California Press, 2001), 82.

9. My analysis of U.S. policy on Filipinos is indebted to Ngai's account in *Impossible Subjects: Illegal Aliens and the Making of Modern America*, 119–26.

10. President McKinley to Secretary of War, 21 December 1899, in Correspondence Relating to the War with Spain, April 15, 1898–July 30, 1902, 2 vols. (Washington, D.C.: 1902), 2: 858–59, quoted in Ngai, *Impossible Subjects: Illegal Aliens and the Making of Modern America*, 99.

11. Vicente Rafael, "'White Love': Surveillance and National Resistance in the U.S. Colonization of the Philippines," in *Cultures of U.S. Imperialism*, eds. Amy Kaplan and Donald E. Pease (Durham, N.C.: Duke University Press), 186–87.

12. For a discussion of the novelties and discontinuities of the "unincorporated" category, see Lanny Thompson, "The Imperial Republic: A Comparison of the Insular Territories under U.S. Dominion after 1898," *Pacific Historical Review* 71, no. 4 (November 2002): 535–74.

13. Letter from Filipino Workers Delegation to Asparagus Growers (February 1928), reprinted in *Stockton Philippine Advertiser*, 29 February 1928; cited in Ngai, *Impossible Subjects*, 107, 304, n. 39.

14. I am adapting Gary Okihiro's important proposal to reconceptualize Asian American history by taking into account the moments in which Asian peoples entered the consciousness of European colonists in North America rather than privileging the arrivals and corporeal presence of Asian groups as the conceptual point of departure for Asian American histories. See *Margins and Mainstreams: Asians in American History and Culture* (Seattle: University of Washington, 1994), 3–30.

15. Carlos Bulosan, *America Is in the Heart: A Personal History* (1946; Seattle: University of Washington Press, 1989), 67. Further references are to this edition and will be cited in parentheses in the text.

16. Kandice Chuh productively reads this scene as a comment on objectification: "Allos objectifies himself as a 'native' to accommodate the colonial gaze, and yet it is that same gaze that teaches him to be ashamed for performing that expected, imposed identity." Kandice Chuh, *Imagine Otherwise: On Asian Americanist Critique* (Durham, N.C.: Duke University Press, 2004), 38.

17. Ngai, *Impossible Subjects: Illegal Aliens and the Making of Modern America*, 111.

18. See Donald Elliot Anthony, "Filipino Labor in California," *Sociology and Social Research* 16, no. 2 (January–February 1931): 156. "Helping to account for this point of view on his part," writes Anthony, "are the following facts: the Filipino owes allegiance to the same flag as the American; American teachers in the Islands have taught him that 'all men are created equal'; he belongs, in most cases, to a class of society which is far above that of the Chinese and the Japanese coolie, and his natural sensitiveness causes him to resent being classed in the same category with them."

19. Donald Anthony, "Filipino Labor in California," 156.

20. Emory Bogardus, *Contemporary Sociology: A Companion Volume to the History of Social Thought* (Los Angeles: University of Southern California Press, 1932), 19.

21. Bogardus, *Contemporary Sociology*, 19.

22. Bulosan is citing *Roldan v. the United States* (1933), in which U.S. federal courts relied upon ethnological studies in the decision to allow the marriage between a Filipino man and Caucasian woman based on the racial classification of Filipinos as Malay rather than Mongolian. But the courts also drew upon scientific studies to amend antimiscegenation statutes to include members of the Malay race. For more on Roldan, see Ngai, *Impossible Subjects*, 115.

23. See Emory S. Bogardus, introduction to *Social Problems and Social Processes: Selected Papers from the Proceedings of the American Sociological Society, 1932* (Chicago: University of Chicago Press, 1933), ix–xii. "To define a social process," writes

Bogardus, "is to describe the series of social changes that the process involves, and most important, the effects that these changes exert upon the attitudes and values of all the persons involved. In this way the significance of a social process becomes vivid. After all, its meaning in human terms is invaluable in the study of social problems" (xi).

24. Emory Bogardus to Fred H. Matthews, 12 September 1963, quoted in Fred H. Matthews, *The Quest for an American Sociology: Robert E. Park and the Chicago School* (Montreal, Quebec, and London, UK: McGill-Queen's University Press, 1977), 114–5.

25. Emory S. Bogardus, "A Social Distance Scale," *Sociology and Social Research* 17 (1933): 265–71; 268.

26. David Lloyd, "Race under Representation," *Oxford Literary Review* 13, nos. 1–2 (1991): 62–94. For readings of Lloyd's essay, see Laura Chrisman, "Theorizing 'Race,' Racism, and Culture: Pitfalls of Idealist Tendencies," *Paragraph: A Journal of Modern Critical Theory* 16, no. 1 (March 1993): 78–90; see also Richard Dyer's use of Lloyd's model of disinterested subjecthood in *White* (London and New York: Routledge, 1997), 38–40.

27. Lloyd, "Race under Representation," 64.

28. Ngai, *Impossible Subjects*, 111.

29. On Luce's containment of New Deal reformism as a strategy of U.S. imperial expansion, see Nikhil Pal Singh, "Culture/Wars: Recoding Empire in an Age of Democracy," *American Quarterly* 50, no. 3 (September 1998): 479.

30. Rachel C. Lee notes how this scene sets up a Filipina as a stylistic device that helps to consolidate Bulosan's multiracial, fraternal vision of community. Written on behalf of a symbolic female figure, this narrative enables Carlos's multiracial fraternal vision of community but also turns on her gendered exclusion. Although I agree with Lee's claim that Bulosan's vision of America as a multiracial fraternal community is secured through both the symbolic presence of women and her exclusion from participation in the community, I also want to take Bulosan's historical intervention into account. See Rachel C. Lee, *The Americas of Asian America: Gendered Fictions of Nation and Transnation* (Princeton, N.J.: Princeton University Press, 1999), 35–36.

31. Ngai, *Impossible Subjects*, 136.

32. James Kyung-Jin Lee challenges conventional conceptions of Asian American model minorities as "models" for "less materially successful groups of color," arguing instead that they are more accurately viewed as figures that "broker the terms through which racial interaction is undertaken, which identities and activities are made legitimate and which are deemed criminal." See James Kyung-Jin Lee, *Urban Triage: Race and the Fictions of Multiculturalism* (Minneapolis: University of Minnesota Press, 2004), 101.

4. Not Black, Not Coolies

1. Jade Snow Wong, *Fifth Chinese Daughter* (Seattle: University of Washington Press, 1989), 244. The significance of the shop window display in Wong's personal narrative is further affirmed by the fact that she offers another account of her live display more than half a century later: "Whenever I stepped into the window, day

or night, I drew crowds of spectators. Chinatown merchants laughed at me for my primitive production, so sure that I was doomed to fail because my pieces were priced higher than mass-produced Chinese porcelain painted with golden dragons." Jade Snow Wong, "The Path to Self-Determination: How I Came to Mills and How It Changed My Life," *Mills Quarterly* 94, no. 1 (Summer 2005): 18–23, 20.

2. Situating Wong's artist–entrepreneur in the contexts of the expansion of a discourse of the immigrant family to Asian Americans complicates our understanding of the dominant Chinese American progress narrative and teleological narratives of postwar U.S. ascendancy. For more on post–World War II Chinese middle-class formation, see Sucheng Chan and Mae Ngai. Chan notes the contemporaneous and intertwined democratic and legal reforms that contributed to Chinese American middle-class hegemony, including the GI Bill, which enabled veterans of Chinese, Japanese, and Filipino ancestry to attend college, become professionals, and become part of an expanding Asian American middle class in urban centers as well as newly integrated areas, as well as the extension of the 1945 War Brides Act to Asian GIs in 1947, which enabled them to bring their Asian brides back to the United States and propelled a drive to buy homes. See Sucheng Chan, *Asian Americans: An Interpretive History* (Boston: Twayne Publishers, 1991). Mae Ngai notes the movement of an expanded and revitalized Chinese American middle class from marginal Chinatown communities to university and suburban communities. See Mae M. Ngai, *Impossible Subjects: Illegal Aliens and the Making of Modern America* (Princeton, N.J.: Princeton University Press, 2005), 203.

3. As Lisa Lowe suggestively writes, "As a figure that promised social order, the Chinese woman was a supplement who appeared to complete the prospective future society of the colony; yet her absence, around which desire was reiterated, marked the limit of a social field whose coherence and closure depended on ideas of racial purity and distinction" (198). Lisa Lowe, "The Intimacies of Four Continents," in *Haunted by Empire: Geographies of Intimacy in North American History*, ed. Ann Laura Stoler (Durham, N.C.: Duke University Press, 2006), 191–212.

4. Remarking on how violent processes of assimilation often accompany notions of U.S. liberation and progress, Lisa Yoneyama argues that, during World War II, transforming the Japanese national polity into a postwar demilitarized nation was symbolized by the granting of full civil rights to Japanese women in the postwar constitution. Lisa Yoneyama, "Liberation under Siege: U.S. Military Occupation and Japanese Women's Enfranchisement," *American Quarterly* 57, no. 3 (September 2005): 885–910.

5. David Palumbo-Liu offers a compelling reading of this scene as the reinscription of Jade Snow into an Old World patriarchal order through her father's story about her artisan grandfather. I argue, however, that the Chinatown "community" that Wong depicts does not refer to a preexisting Old World, but is rather an emergent formation. See David Palumbo-Liu, *Asian/American: Historical Crossings of a Racial Frontier* (Palo Alto, Calif.: Stanford University Press, 1996), 144.

6. Moon-Ho Jung argues that by the 1880s, "alongside the prostitute, there was no more potent symbol of chattel slavery's enduring legacy than the 'coolie,' a racialized and racializing figure that anti-Chinese (and putatively pro-Chinese) lawmakers

condemned." See Moon-Ho Jung, "Outlawing 'Coolies': Race, Nation, and Empire in the Age of Emancipation," *American Quarterly* 37, no. 3 (September 2005): 677–701, 678, 698.

7. See Devlin on how postwar books of advice may have been more explicit and forward thinking on sexual matters, but they also framed these issues within the narrow scope of family relationships and parents' homes rather than in relation to a "broader notion of independence as a major goal of female adolescence" (117). Rachel Devlin, *Relative Intimacy: Fathers, Adolescent Daughters, and Postwar American Culture* (Chapel Hill: University of North Carolina Press, 2005), 131.

8. Here, I want to suggest that the discourse on coolies was not unidirectional. Rather, Chinese Americans such as Jade Snow Wong could take up the dichotomy of coolies and immigrants and adapt it not only to contest assumptions of their foreignness but also to make their cultural production more acceptable within an atmosphere of anticommunism.

9. Lieutenant Edward Duran Ayres of the Los Angeles sheriff's department draws on biological racism based on genetics to make a case for the racial determinants for Mexican juvenile delinquency. In his grand jury testimony for the Sleepy Lagoon case, also known as the Ayres Report, Ayres attributes Mexican criminality to the "oriental background" of the pre-Columbian inhabitants of Mexico. Mauricio Mazon, *The Zoot Suit Riots: The Psychology of Social Alienation* (Austin: University of Texas Press, 1984), 22.

10. See Stuart Cosgrove, "The Zoot Suit and Style Warfare," *History Workshop Journal* 18, no. 1 (1984): 77–91.

11. Catherine S. Ramírez, "Crimes of Fashion: The Pachuca and Chicana Style Politics," *Meridians* 2, no. 2 (2002): 1–35; 7.

12. In particular, the repeal of exclusion laws rendered Chinese immigration "legitimate," ending a racist policy that had been in effect for sixty years and enabling Chinese to naturalize as citizens. An important component of the repeal was that it paved the way for non-quota family migration, thus giving the nuclear family and notions of "respectable domesticity" even more significance as the criteria by which Chinese Americans would continue to be measured and deemed acceptable as potential citizens. As Nayan Shah observes, the shift in the dominant image of Chinatown from a vice-ridden, diseased slum to a tourist destination for white middle-class families parallels changing conceptions of Chinatown's inhabitants from a bachelor society of working-class men and women to a society of nuclear-family households. The legal enfranchisement and cultural elevation of Chinese as "legitimate immigrants" and "deserving citizens" was thus intertwined with the emphasis on ideologies of family and respectable domesticity. Nayan Shah, *Contagious Divides: Epidemics and Race in San Francisco's Chinatown* (Berkeley: University of California Press, 2001), 225.

13. Robert Lee notes that white and immigrant American workers drew upon the myth of the Chinese coolie laborer to racialize and define a particular sector of wage labor as wage slavery. By insisting upon a natural division between "coolie" wage slavery and free labor, white workers could claim that a "semi-artisan status" was reserved for whites: "The myth of the Chinese coolie laborer allowed white American workers, both native born and immigrant, to racialize a stratum of wage work equated

with wage slavery while reserving for whites a semi-artisan status." Robert G. Lee, *Orientals: Asian Americans in Popular Culture* (Philadelphia, Pa.: Temple University Press, 1999), 61.

14. As Robin Kelley notes, "Demographic and economic transformations caused by the war not only intensified racial conflict but led to heightened class tensions within urban black communities." Robin D. G. Kelley, "The Riddle of the Zoot," in *Race Rebels: Culture, Politics, and the Black Working Class* (New York: The Free Press, 1994), 165.

15. Ngai, *Impossible Subjects*, 8.

16. Ibid., 169–70.

17. Lee, *Orientals*, 3.

18. For an informative, if somewhat idealized, account of the GI Bill, or Servicemen's Readjustment Act of 1944, see Michael J. Bennett, *When Dreams Came True: The GI Bill and the Making of Modern America* (Washington, D.C., and London, UK: Brassey's, 1996).

19. Remarking on the centrality of the figure of the "Chinatown bachelor," Elaine Kim writes, "Chinatown life was largely organized around the needs of these womanless, childless men who had been segregated from participation in the mainstream of American life by race discrimination" (91). Elaine Kim, "Portraits of Chinatown," in *Asian American Literature: An Introduction to the Writings and Their Social Context* (Philadelphia, Pa.: Temple University Press, 1982), 91–121. Mary Lui also points out how the critical emphasis on the effects of immigrant exclusion laws shaped conceptualizations of Chinatowns as "insular bachelor societies," but also advanced historical narratives that define ethnic and racial homogeneity and solidarity as the criterion for community, thus erasing and silencing those who could not claim Chinese descent nor mixed parentage. Mary Ting Yi Lui, *The Chinatown Trunk Murder Mystery: Murder, Miscegenation, and Other Dangerous Encounters in Turn-of-the-Century New York* (Princeton, N.J.: Princeton University Press, 2004), 11.

20. According to Christina Klein, these books assumed that there was no longer a rationale for racial exclusion since postwar American society had adopted an ideology of cultural pluralism and could thus deploy spectacular and touristic displays of ethnic culture to articulate Chineseness as culture and in turn produce a different version of Chinatown than nineteenth-century representations that underscored its absolute foreignness. Christina M. Klein, *Cold War Orientalism: Asia in the Middlebrow Imagination, 1945–1961* (Berkeley: University of California Press, 2003), 228.

21. Klein, *Cold War Orientalism*, 241.

22. As Mae Ngai argues, "The 'other' is not a passive body appropriated by hegemonic discourse, but a social actor—one operating within constraints set by structures and relations of power, to be sure, but nonetheless a social actor in pursuit of his or her own agenda." Mae M. Ngai, "Transnationalism and the Transformation of the 'Other,'" *American Quarterly* 57, no. 1 (2005): 59–65, 61.

23. Kim, "Portraits of Chinatown," 92.

24. Ibid., 47.

25. Luce defines the measure of U.S. "virility" in terms of the United States' ability to exploit Asia: "Our thinking today on world trade today is on ridiculously small

terms. For example, we think of Asia as being worth only a few hundred millions a year to us. Actually, in the decades to come Asia will be worth to us exactly zero—or it will be worth to us four, five, ten billions of dollars a year. And the latter are the terms we must think in, or else confess a pitiful impotence." Reprinted in Henry R. Luce, "The American Century," *Diplomatic History* 23, no. 2 (spring 1999): 159–71, 171.

26. Luce, "The American Century," 170.

27. Quoted in Klein, 251. Klein observes that, in the nineteenth and early twentieth century, geography was critical for Americans in search of an accessible route to China. Yet in the second part of the twentieth century, Hawaii's Asian population represented the possibility of gaining access to Asian markets and resources.

28. Him Mark Lai focuses on Chinese students in the United States who were drawn, across class lines, to idealism of Chinese communists and disillusionment with Chinese Nationalist government. Writing against the notion of unified Chinese diaspora consciousness, he considers leftist students who want to return to rebuild China during the cold war. Him Mark Lai, "The Chinese-Marxist Left, Chinese Students, and Scholars in America, and the New China: Mid-1940s to Mid-1950s," *Chinese America: History and Perspectives* 18 (2004): 7–26.

29. Shirley J. Lim, *A Feeling of Belonging: Asian American Women's Public Culture* (New York: New York University Press, 2006), 131.

30. The accompanying text reads: "Jade Snow Wong, using an arm rest, throws a vase on the potter's wheel. The artist has exhibited her exquisite ceramics nationwide. Several pieces are among the collections at New York's Museum of Modern Art and Metropolitan Museum of Art. Miss Wong wrote a bestseller, *Fifth Chinese Daughter*." Franc Shor, "Boom on San Francisco Bay," *National Geographic Magazine* 110, no. 2 (August 1956): 211.

31. As part of an article on the rapidly developing San Francisco Bay area, *National Geographic* published a photograph of Wong at her pottery wheel, above the caption "An Ancient Art of China Finds Modern Expression." Although Wong was positioned as a cold war endorsement of capitalist accumulation practices, she also continued to be represented as external to conventional definitions of U.S. workers and the national body. Wong's live display and representation in popular magazines also needs to be read in the context of contemporaneous associations of Japanese women with aberrant domesticity and enslavement and hence with a culture in need of reform. Robert Lee also notes that white and immigrant American workers drew upon the "myth of the Chinese coolie laborer" to racialize a particular sector of wage labor and define it as wage slavery. By insisting upon a natural division between coolie wage slavery and free labor, white workers could claim that a "semi-artisan status" was reserved for whites. Robert G. Lee, *Orientals: Asian Americans in Popular Culture* (Philadelphia, Pa.: Temple University Press, 1999), 61.

32. Jade Snow Wong, "Puritans from the Orient: A Chinese Evolution," in *The Immigrant Experience: The Anguish of Becoming American*, ed. Thomas C. Wheeler (New York: Dial Press, 1971), 128.

33. See Henry Yu, *Thinking Orientals: Migration, Contact, and Exoticism in Modern America* (New York: Oxford University Press, 2001), 97.

34. Robert Park writes, "The Japanese bears in his features a distinctive racial hallmark . . . a racial uniform that classifies him." Robert E. Park, "Racial Assimi-

lation in Secondary Groups, with Particular Reference to the Negro," in *Race and Culture: The Collected Writings of Robert Ezra Park* (Glencoe, Ill.: The Free Press, 1950), 208–9.

35. Yu, *Thinking Orientals*.

36. Leti Volpp, "Divesting Citizenship: On Asian American History and the Loss of Citizenship through Marriage," *UCLA Law Review* 52 (December 2005): 4.

37. Prashad investigates what he identifies as the convergence of pluralist multiculturalism with an ideology of upward mobility that results in a "culture of upwardly mobile racialism." Vijay Prashad, Foreword: "Bandung Is Done: Passages in Afro-Asian Epistemology," in *AfroAsian Encounters: Culture, History, Politics*, eds. Heike Raphael-Hernandez and Shannon M. Steen (New York: New York University Press, 2006), xvii.

Coda

1. Chellen et al. and *EEOC v. John Pickle Company, Inc.*, Case No. 02-CV-0085-CVE-FHM [Base File] and 02-CV-0979-CVE-FHM [Consolidated]. U.S. District Court for the Northern District of Oklahoma. May 2006.

2. *National Public Radio*, "This American Life," Episode 344, "The Competition" (November 30, 2007).

3. The characterization of the case in terms of the American dream transformed into a nightmare is also attributed to Tom Brokaw on the "NBC Nightly News." See John Bowe, *Nobodies: Modern American Slave Labor and the Dark Side of the New Economy* (New York: Random House, 2007), 180.

4. Bowe, *Nobodies*, 180.

5. John Bowe interview, *National Public Radio*, "This American Life," Episode 344, "The Competition" (November 30, 2007).

6. Bowe, *Nobodies*, 149.

Index

Cynthia H. Tolentino is assistant professor of English at the University of Oregon.